Marcham Pub

I0072410

The Executive Secretary Guide to Conference and Event Management

Eth Lloyd

M.Ed. NDBA, AAPNZ (Life, Fellow, Cert.)

I wish to dedicate this book to all administrative professionals who are so often asked to do really skilled tasks, which they manage well, without any of the formal training that so many others in the office receive.

This book is for you.

Foreword

I would like to recommend Eth Lloyd's writing on "Successful Conference and Event Management"to all administrative professionals. I have worked with Eth Lloyd for a number of years on various events and as many of you know, organising any event is a challenge, but can also be very rewarding.

Eth has had vast experience in the organisation of events, one being the World Administrators Summit in Papua New Guinea in 2015. Eth is testament to using technology at its full potential as she resides in New Zealand and worked with a co-chair in Port Moresby for the International Summit and co-ordinating an international advisory committee. She is currently Chairman of the International Advisory Council, managing the preparation for the World Administrators Summit in Frankfurt, Germany in 2018.

I have held the positions of National President of the Australian Institute of Office Professionals, Inaugural Chair of the International Advisory Committee for the International Summit and a Director of International Association of Administrative Professionals.

This book is a must for your bookshelf for ready and quick access!

Leanne Fisher
GradCert (Bus) FAIOP HLMAIOP MAICD

Contents

Introduction

Almost every administrative professional carries out event management. This may be for a small event such as a staff farewell or retirement right through to a large international event with invited speakers and paying attendees. They are all events, and administrative professionals are capably managing these events every day without any formal training, demonstrating skills and knowledge built up by quite simply doing the job.

Event management is a type of project management. If we understand the principles behind project management and apply them to event management, we can do the task more efficiently.

This book does not claim to be a guide to successful project management. It uses project management tools to support more efficient and effective management of events that you, as an administrative professional, may be asked to arrange.

The first chapter outlines briefly the tools and terminology of project management. Chapters two to six apply those project management tools to managing events. The final chapter relates a series of real-life experiences of managing events.

There is value in using project management tools as they will provide even more control of your event. Having everything under control means that if you are suddenly unavailable leading up to the event or on the day, everything is in good order and someone else can step easily into the job. The worst thing we can be is indispensable as that puts the most inordinate amount of pressure on us.

I worked in the administrative profession for 30 years and have also been involved in my own professional association for 20 years. In my work, I often managed events of varying sizes, however it was a "Project management for administrative assistants" training course which changed how I did things. I quickly saw how I could manage events, being pro-active rather than reactive, by doing planning up front rather than getting into the detail before I saw the whole picture and thereby forestalling some problems.

Being a Co-Convenor of the Stars 2000 week-long international event with Tricia Caughley tested and grew those skills. Then 10 years as a Director of AAPNZ Professional Development Ltd (AAPNZ PDL) with oversight and responsibility for AAPNZ's Annual Conference. These events were hosted by a local AAPNZ

Group, but the financial responsibility for each event rested with AAPNZ PDL.

I was deeply involved in running the 2011 International Office Professionals Summit which was hosted by AAPNZ, as part of the International Advisory Council, the Host Country Team, and also as a Director of AAPNZ PDL. All of those roles involved working with volunteers which provides its own specific challenges (see Tricia Caughley's real-life experience of working with volunteers in Chapter 7).

Since 2005 I have been a member of the World Administrators Summit (WASummit) Advisory Council with oversight of the WASummit preparations and planning. This is another whole level of challenge and satisfaction with volunteers who are spread over several countries.

What I have learnt over the years is that "good management" (planning, documentation, oversight (monitoring and control), debriefing) and **not** "good luck" are what lead to a successful event.

> ## "GOOD MANAGEMENT, NOT GOOD LUCK"
> ### should be your motto.

Eth Lloyd
M.Ed., P.G.Dip. Ed., NDBA, AAPNZ (Life, Fellow, Cert)

1

Project Management

There are many books, on-line information, and training courses available on project management. To become skilled in project management you need to undertake learning at many different levels.

What is a project?

A project is a task which has a defined start date, specified end dates and is usually of a duration great enough to require formal planning.

While project management was commonly used for IT or other large projects it is now used for a wide variety of projects. However, the principles of project management are useful in a wide range of situations, including helping with efficiency, control and effectiveness of event management and many other tasks that administrative professionals carry out.

Terminology in project management

There are various terms which relate to project management. These terms may not apply to every project but they are common to most projects. These terms include:

Life cycle – there are six different phases of a project. In some form or another all projects run with this life cycle.

1. initiation – the starting point

2. scope/definition – the bigger picture

3. planning – the details

4. control/monitoring – ongoing oversight

5. implementation – the project goes live

6. review or debrief – the wrap-up

Project brief/plan – this is the initial plan of the project and sets out the objectives. It may include a range of general items such as overall purpose, who the initiators are, a desired implementation time and major influences.

Scope – is a statement which gives an overview of the project and shows a link to the overall business plan. It sets out what is in and out of scope, what is to be achieved, and the size of the project.

Scope creep – this happens when the size of the task increases without proper planning, acknowledgement, or recognition of the effects on implementation and success. Uncontrolled scope creep can lead to a project failing in many areas from financial to implementation.

Project administrator – in larger projects a dedicated project administrator takes responsibility for managing documentation and recording. This may be an opportunity to step into project work and there are some specific training courses for this role.

Project co-ordinator – in larger projects a project co-ordinator takes some of the responsibility from the project manager. This can be a career move for a project administrator and there are specific training courses for this role. This role may lead on to project management.

Project manager –the person who has overall day-to-day responsibility for the project and owns it in daily detail.

Project sponsor –the person who gives the project to the project manager; she or he owns the project at a high level. This person could be the CEO or a director of a company, a stakeholder or another senior executive or manager.

Phases in project management – Life cycle

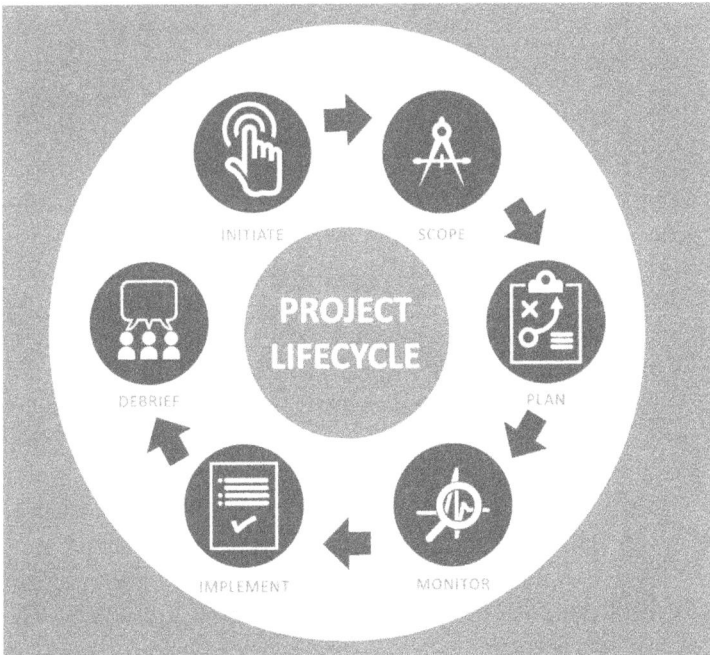

Initiation – when the project is given out, why it is needed, potential budget and its aims. It may include a description of the issue or task to be worked on or perhaps an opportunity to be exploited and whether there is a deadline by which the result is needed. The project manager will produce a project brief from the initiation meeting and this brief will be further developed in the scope/definition phase.

Scope/Definition – defining the scope of the project, what it is expected to deliver and why, can often be the most important part of planning. Scope definition largely deals with the bigger picture issues to ensure project delivery. It is also when budget figures are considered. Understanding the scope of the project is critical to ensure that what has been asked for is being provided, and that all are alert to the possibility of "scope creep" (see above).

Planning – time spent planning up front will hugely reduce the possibility of disasters, stress and failure. The more time spent on scope/definition, budgeting and planning the better; a project can run into difficulties when those tasked with running it get into the detail too soon and miss important aspects (such as risk assessment and mitigation) due to not having gathered the wider overall picture.

Monitoring/Control and Reporting – this is when the project manager reviews project progress against budget and the timeline/schedule and reports progress to the project sponsor noting any variances and remedial action to be taken.

Monitoring ensures that there are no surprises and that every unexpected event is picked up either before it happens or immediately it happens so that any remedial action or accommodation can occur. Having a "no surprises" approach will help enormously to ensure the project will be completed on time and in budget.

Good documentation is an important part of a project lifecycle and one aspect of that is reporting. These reports, developed over the whole of the project, will spell out the whole story of the project. Sound documentation will enable someone else to pick up the project if the project manager is unable to finish the task.

> **NOTE** Good documentation, including reporting, sets out the whole story of the project.

Implementation – this can be the fun part; it is when all the above steps come to fruition and lead to a successful outcome. However, good planning will ensure the implementation occurs on time and in budget.

Debrief/Review – is when all of those involved in the project review whether the objectives were met, the successes, lessons learnt, things to avoid and generally "put the project to bed". It is when all of those involved in the project can discuss their experiences and so feel that there has been a fitting end to the project.

Providing and receiving feedback can be quite challenging, especially if you have not had previous good experiences. One method of managing this is to use the "Stop – Keep Doing – Start model" for oral feedback[1].

Understanding this process will help you to provide constructive and useful feedback and, importantly, to receive it as well.

---

[1]https://www.mindtools.com/pages/article/SKS-process.htm

Tools commonly used in project management

- Spreadsheets – timeline
- Gantt Charts
- Specialist project management software
- In-house project management tools
- Various documentation mostly as required by your organisation:
  - project reports
  - minutes of project meetings
  - budget reports
  - in many cases timesheets for those involved in the project
  - expenses/invoices
  - variance reports.

2

Event Management

What is an event?

An event can be anything from the office social party through to a major international conference with fee-paying attendees and high profile speakers.

One person might readily manage small events essentially on their own, for example yourself with support from the event sponsor. However, larger events will mostly require a team of two or more, e.g. you and your team. Alternatively, they might be handled by a specialist event manager or Professional Conference Organiser (PCO). However, even if you have taken on a PCO or Event Manager (sometimes also called the Convener), the ultimate responsibility still lies with you, therefore you must be involved with and keep up with everything that is happening.

Is an event a project?

Yes, an event is a project; it has a specified start and end time. The same life cycle that is found in any project applies to running an event though some of the words used might be a little different.

Tools to use in event management

These tools are similar to those used in general project management:

- 'To Do' list (usually with a smaller event, e.g. a staff member farewell)

- Notes in a diary or calendar (usually with a smaller event, e.g. a small cocktail party)

- Electronic project management tool, e.g.

  - specifically developed spreadsheet (see Appendix B)

  - project management software

  - specialised event management tool such as used by event management companies

- In-house project management tools

- Documentation including reports – financial, variance, meeting minutes

- Files and folders

Phases in event management – Life cycle

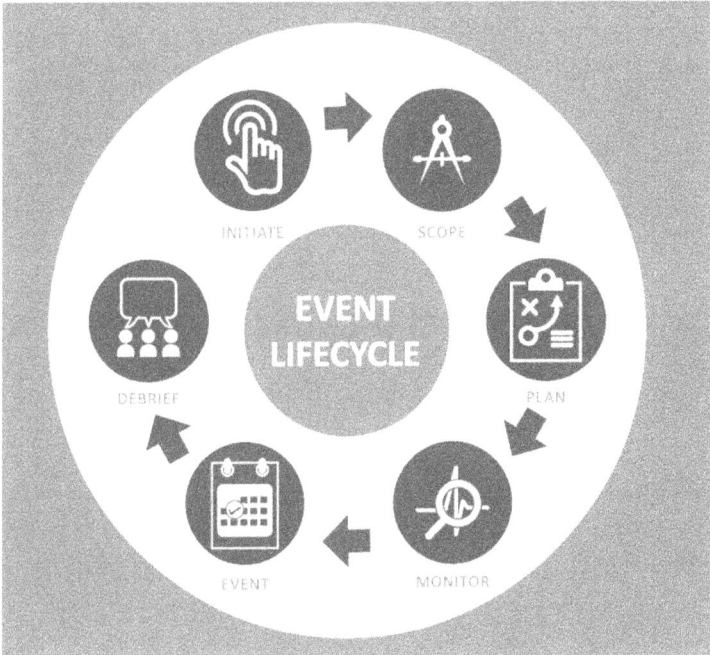

Roles in Event Management

Event Sponsor – who initiates or starts the whole process by asking you to arrange an event.

Event Manager (you) – who needs to monitor progress (planning, expenses against budget, reporting) and ensure the event is held (implementation). The event manager should also always hold a debrief meeting and produce a report, after the event has finished.

Event Team – These are the people you will work with in managing this event. On some occasions, you and the Event Sponsor may be the team. However, you will work with others on specific parts, for example the venue Event Manager, catering specialists, and developing a budget with someone from finance. These all contribute to your team. On other occasions, you will have a defined team of people who you have selected or who have been seconded or delegated to work with you. This may include a professional conference organiser (PCO).

Professional Conference Organiser (PCO)

A PCO is an excellent option if your event is large and where there are no others available to form a team with you, or your organisation cannot commit people to the task. A PCO can also be the right choice if the event requires something special in theming, social events, decorations or other specialist items. A PCO can offer:

- project management skills

- creativity and new ideas

- the ability to focus specifically on the event, freeing up staff within the organisation to continue to do their day-to-day jobs or, if the event is to only be one part of the project, undertake their own part of that project

- management of the budget

- connections to get better prices from suppliers

- specialist conference registration software which can be crucial if the event is large, has a registration fee and requires full financial management.

There are many PCOs in the market and research is required to find one who fits with you, your organisation and its values and your event requirements. Make sure you ask for referees and contact them for comment. Do note that using a PCO can be quite a high cost item so be sure that you have the budget to handle that.

Be sure all parties are clear on the objective(s) being worked towards right from the start; this is particularly important as a PCO introduces to the project another level of responsibility and therefore opportunity for misunderstanding.

It is critical that you meet with your event sponsor and the PCO together to ensure the event objectives are clear and you are all in agreement. Such a meeting can also provide you with an opportunity to further clarify understanding of the objectives by having a third party ask different questions.

When working with a PCO you need to:

- Develop a brief (this may be a similar brief to the one you developed as soon as you were asked to manage the event (initiation) but with details specific to the PCO)

- Define the scope of work to be done by the PCO

  - Are they handling your registrations?

  - Are they handling the event finances?

  - Are they working with you on sponsorship?

  - Are they responsible for theming your Gala Dinner?

  - Are you expecting them to come up with social activity ideas and how these might be implemented?

  - Are they handling all or just one or some parts of the event?

- Agree on the price, given what the scope covers and include all details in the contract which must be signed off *before* any actual work starts

- Ask to see the PCO's detailed project plan so all expectations are clarified and delivered

- Hold regular review meetings with the PCO

- Be honest always

- Ensure any major changes are signed off by the event sponsor

- Ensure that timeframes are kept to.

You may decide that a PCO is only required for some aspects of your event management or they may be required for all aspects. You need to:

- determine what your needs are

- determine what budget there is to cover the PCO costs and how that fits in with other costs the organisation might be covering

- make sure their costs do not take up all the budget

- discuss and agree how your requirements will be met by the PCO

- be clear on the boundaries between you, the event manager and the PCO, particularly areas of responsibility.

It is important that a PCO fits with you, your organisation and its values and your event requirements. Be sure everyone, including the PCO, are clear on the objective(s) being worked towards. Make sure where the PCO is used for only part of the event management that their costs do not use all the budget. Carefully clarify boundaries for responsibilities between the PCO and you, the event manager.

Remember: the three key factors in your relationship with the PCO are
Definition, Planning and Communication

3

Initiation and Scoping

The initiation phase is when you are asked, by the event sponsor, to arrange the event. You then become the event manager/convener.

If you fully understand the initiation and spend time to carefully scope the event, then all other phases have a sound foundation to work from.

The scoping phase is when you start building your event brief (see Appendix A). Ensure you are clear about the requirements and the aims/objective(s) of your event. In many ways, this is the most important phase of your event. This is when you determine the backing and resources for the event from your event sponsor and you agree on what the successful event will look like.

> **NOTE** Scope – to fully understand what you are being asked to do, focus on the "whats" and "whys" etc. of your event before getting into the detail.

Asking the right questions and recording the answers will form the basis of your event brief and planning. This is when you answer some of the big questions: who is managing it, who is attending, etc. as set out in the following table.

The right questions to ask – help to define the scope/definition[2]	
Why?	Why is the event being held?
What?	What outcome(s) is (are) expected? What type of event – drinks, conference, breakfast, whole day, part day, etc.?
Where?	Where is the event to be held – location? Where is the event to be held – type of venue?
How?	How is it to be funded? How many might attend? How might attendees get there?
Who?	Who is to manage it – in-house, PCO, mix of both? Who is expected to attend? Who might support/sponsor it? Who might be presenting at it?
When?	When is the event to be held?

If possible, request the time (perhaps a week or two) to primarily focus on this part of the event.

[2]Table modified from the book – Dorling Kindersley Ltd Essential Managers Project Management

Getting this part right will make a significant difference to the success of your event. Any misunderstandings or gaps you pick up later must be corrected or added part way through, always at some cost to the budget, timeline or levels of stress and dissatisfaction.

Who is your Event Sponsor?

The first thing required is to clarify who is driving this event: who is the event sponsor? Is it the manager or CEO, is it a Director or President of the organisation who has asked for the event to be arranged? Is it your manager? Find out who is behind the event and therefore who has control of the resources and has the final authority. This information gives you a better understanding of what is at stake and to whom you will ultimately be reporting.

Understanding who is behind the event quite naturally leads to why the event is being run and indicates how important the event is to your organisation. Always be honest with the event sponsor to help eliminate any surprises.

> **NOTE** Avoid surprises – do not hide errors or mistakes even if the error is serious and is yours.

Why is this event being held?

The reason why an event is being held will often determine the type of event, the venue type, the formality, the target audience, the agenda or programme, etc. Understanding why your event is being held is critical to your understanding what type of event you are being asked to deliver.

Example: the event might be to launch a new product. The reason for this event will help to determine what type of event is required and who the target audience is. For some new products this might be something very big and making a statement, for others it might be rather more low key but with very specific attendees for whom this product is important.

> **NOTE** Clarify the answers to why your event is being held before you consider any details.

What type of event?

Now you know why the event is being held, the next step is to determine what type of event is being asked for.

Example: product launch. Questions to ask:

- Is it to be a small cocktail party, an exhibition, part of a conference or a large theatrical presentation such as for a new iPhone?

- Is it a combination of one or more of those options to reach different markets?

- Is it to be held in an in-house venue or externally?

- Is it a smaller but none the less important event such as a drinks reception, a dinner, or a breakfast meeting?

The type of event corresponds very closely to why the event is being held and may be answered at the same time. However, always ask the questions because, while it may initially appear to be one thing when the question is "why?", the type of event to be held may require something different when the question is "what type?".

The type of event will determine the processes and the time frame required to set it up – a drinks reception can be arranged in a far shorter time than an international conference with prestigious international speakers. Understanding what type of event is required quite naturally leads to who will be attending.

Who will be in your Team?

The team to manage your event may be a team of you and the event sponsor or there may be several people on the team. A team of two may require extra people along the way or to manage the actual event.

For any event your team may be built through selecting those who have the time available and an interest in working on the event rather than specific skills. Sometimes your team will be built by people being delegated/seconded to be involved with little choice. When building a team, look for people's strengths so they are asked to do a role they can do well; this will make a significant difference to your team's effectiveness.

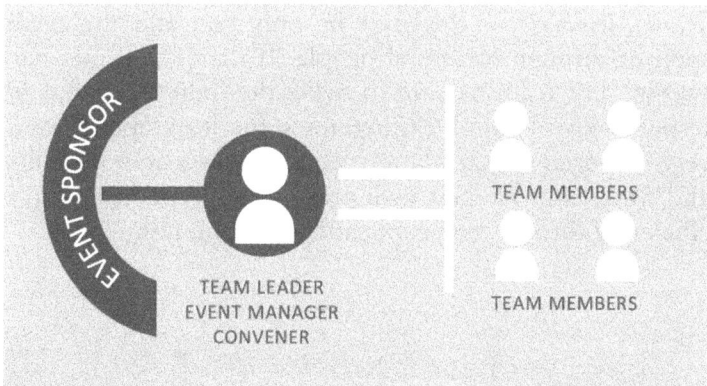

EVENT SPONSOR

TEAM LEADER
EVENT MANAGER
CONVENER

TEAM MEMBERS

TEAM MEMBERS

Team Roles

Event sponsor – as described above

Team Leader (may also be referred to as Event Manager or Convener) – this is the role that many administrative professionals take on, often without their recognising it as such. This role has the day-to-day responsibility for the event, reports to the event sponsor and fully understands the objective(s) of the event, the budget, the timeframe and the requirements (venue, speakers, programme, food, registration, etc.).

If you, as Team Leader, have a team of people to work with, then being an effective communicator and motivator and having strong time management and organisational skills will be very important.

The initial meeting of your event team should include the Event Sponsor, who must identify your delegated authority levels (as the Team Leader/Event Manager). This can be important if some on your team have a higher position in the organisation than you, to ensure you are clearly identified as the leader of this team in this situation.

Team Member(s) – this may be only you and the event sponsor through to several people. If there are more than two in your team be sure to make the individual areas of responsibility clear. Defining roles for team members is very important as it allows people to take responsibility and ownership of their own areas. It also uses time more efficiently through not duplicating work on tasks.

Event Brief

Scope is the phase where you develop the context for the event and understand the higher-level picture which will be captured in your event brief. Your event brief must clearly set out what is expected, how it is to be delivered and defines the objective(s).

Your brief will record changes to the event, which in turn allows you to manage scope creep. It also ensures everyone knows that there have been additions or changes to the initial request.

Take time to evaluate any changes you are asked to or must make to the initial brief, before getting sign-off. Never hesitate to outline potential risks (e.g. budget blow-out if additional or more expensive activities are requested). Note these risks and any remedial action in the brief and then get sign-off. Risks can lead to change and changes can sometimes make delivery more difficult, therefore ensuring any change is noted and signed off is an important part of the audit trail.

Scope creep[3] is a term used to describe uncontrolled changes to the scope of a project. The term 'creep' is used because the changes happen in such small steps that they may go unnoticed until their true impact becomes apparent close to implementation. It can be caused by the event manager failing to spot holes in the initial brief or by the event sponsor changing his/her mind on one or more factors.

---

[3]Dorling Kindersley Ltd Essential Managers Project Management, p. 74

Documentation

Various specific documents will assist you in managing planning for the event. Most often using your organisation's own documentation, perhaps with some adjustment, will be sufficient.

The types of documentation you require might include:

1. Event Brief – including:

    a. objectives

    b. milestones

    c. risks and mitigation suggestions

    d. sign-off space

2. Budget (hyperlink to it in the event brief)

3. Timeline

4. PCO brief if you are using a PCO

5. Meeting documentation including:

    a. Agenda

    b. Minutes

6. Reporting format to event sponsor including debrief report

7. Financial variance reports

You should create an event folder in either hard or soft copy or both, where everything to do with the event is held under your control. Note, if your event folder is in soft copy only then it must be in a shared space so others can access it, especially if you are unexpectedly unable to continue with the role. It will save you time if you use in-house documentation. However, if it isn't suitable you should develop something specific to meet the needs of your event.

NOTE If your folder is in hard copy consider using different colour paper for each of the different document types so that they are quickly located in your project folder.

Include a footer in your documentation with the file reference, version number and the date and time the document was created to ensure you always know you are working with the most recent version.

What are my budget and financial responsibilities?

It is critical to find out right at the start what sort of budget you have available. The event sponsor may give you an overall figure at initiation and therefore the event budget must fit within that figure. You might have to start from scratch with your budget and build it up as you gather an idea of costs, then have that amount approved, or you might have a previous budget amount to work with.

Is the event to be self-funding, i.e. are the fees expected to cover costs?

If the event is to have paid registrations then determining how many are likely to attend, along with some indicative costs (venue, food, speakers, AV, etc.) will allow you to work out an approximate cost per-head. It is vital you conservatively estimate the number of attendees at this stage. It is very easy to allow enthusiasm for your event to overcome rational judgment. Being conservative in your estimates is the best methodology.

Some of your costs will be fixed, e.g. the cost for the room is likely to be set regardless of the number of attendees (noting of course that the room will have a fixed number it can carry), but catering will fluctuate with the number of attendees as it will be calculated per head.

Once a per-head cost has been determined, profit required (if any) and a contingency amount can be factored in to determine the registration fee. Calculating the registration fee and the likely attendee numbers will provide the anticipated total amount of money available to be worked with.

Example: a voluntary organisation arranged an annual conference with fee-paying attendees. This event had been held for many years and so the organisation involved had a good idea of how many people were likely to attend. This number was regularly between 80 and 120. The new event manager did not wish to be "held back by previous learnings" and wished to budget for 300 attendees. This gave considerable income and allowed for a higher spend on the event. To manage these different expectations, the event manager was asked to do three budgets, one for 80 attendees, one for 120 attendees and one for 300 attendees. Each budget also had identified items which could be cut out as the income reduced so that each budget still "broke-even". As registrations came in it became clear which level of budget was to be worked with.

Be sure you know right from the start what level of financial authorisation you have and who will sign-off if an amount is above your authorisation level.

> **Warning: *This is critical*** – If finance is not your
> strength, seek help from your finance department or
> another appropriate source so that your budget is robust.
>
> Example: a marvellous ceremony that goes way over
> budget is a failure for the event manager, e.g. some of
> the Olympics.

Be sure you know the processes required by your organisation
to contract services; i.e. how many quotes are required, who
the preferred suppliers are, etc., and who must sign-off and
at what level of expenditure.

Risk Analysis

Risk analysis is often overlooked when planning an event.
Risks might be picked up close to implementation when
it is too late to manage them effectively. Risk analysis is
so important it must be part of the scoping phase for the
event. There are two important criteria in evaluating risk:
the probability of something happening, and the impact on
the event if it does.

Risk analysis should be noted in your Event Brief
(Appendix A) to show that risks have been considered
and remedial action thought through. For example: risk
analysis might highlight that due to having an international
speaker there is a need for full event cancellation or speaker
cancellation insurance and perhaps a back-up presenter.

Dealing with risk has five options, these are:

1. *Prevention* – not always possible but involves considering
doing things differently

> **Example:** if the time of year and location pose a risk with travel due to weather, then consider either changing the time of year or the location; this would remove the risk.

2. *Transfer* – perhaps spread the risk

> **Example:** using the same example above stay with the location but provide several ways of travel – air, car, train.

3. *Plan contingency* – Plan B, an alternative that will achieve the same result

> **Example:** if a speaker is suddenly delayed, have an alternative activity or swap speaking slots/lunch (if possible) to fill a vacant slot in the programme. Maybe have a back-up speaker who can fill in at short notice.

4. *Reduce* – either the possibility or the impact of the risk

> **Example**: close management and overview of the finances will reduce the risk of cost overruns – the risk is there but the possibility or impact has been reduced.

5. *Accept* – sometimes the risk is worth accepting

> **Example:** an Act of God may occur but while you can plan for it you cannot know that it will happen so there is nothing that can be done to prevent it.

It is especially important when there are guest speakers/ performers or other outside involvement (e.g. paying attendees), that you have a Plan B in place. This might involve:

- having a back-up speaker or a back-up activity

- the ability to switch speakers around if someone is unexpectedly unavailable for their scheduled time slot but could be available later or earlier.

Thinking through various scenarios means that if they then arise, you are already part way to a solution and plans can be switched smoothly.

The event must be examined for risks and recommended remedial action should be included as part of the event brief (see Appendix A). These may be added as they are discovered, but always raise them with the event sponsor and get agreement/sign-off for the remedial action.

There are always risks. For example, if the event is in a different location from where your organisation is usually based, there can be weather or transport issues which affect many of those attending; what plans can you put in place to handle this if it occurred? If different cultures are involved, e.g. speakers or attendees from overseas they may have different expectations, food or accommodation needs. These must be discussed and agreed to.

If speakers are travelling to your event, to mitigate risk it may be necessary for them to arrive at least the day before they speak, especially if they are international. This will give them time to get over jetlag and to see the venue. If they are local, it may still be best for them to arrive the day before, again to ensure they are comfortable with the venue and logistics on the day.

Be wary of a speaker who thinks they can turn up immediately prior to their presentation. The strain of awaiting their arrival and the knowledge that something could happen will be high and as we all know "if something can go wrong, it will". This would be a significant risk factor and mitigating that risk would be to only agree to speakers/entertainers arriving at an acceptable and agreed time before they are due on stage.

What about "Acts of God"? While these cannot be predicted, this is an excellent time to consider the "What if…?" type scenario. Major weather events are more common now than they seemed to be in the past so the time of year might be important. This type of event might also impact on whether insurance is required or not and what that might cover.

> **Example:** See the real-life experience from Robyn Bennett in Chapter 7 to see how she handled this when a severe earthquake struck just prior to a conference involving 100+ paying attendees, and the subsequent aftershocks.

Health and Safety

Be sure to confirm what responsibilities you as event organiser have with regards to Health and Safety in your country. Some countries have very clear lines of responsibility for different aspects of the event – yours, the venue, etc. You must factor this in, and the time of risk analysis is a good opportunity.

Who will be presenting?

Keynote Speaker

The presenter of a keynote address can make or break an event. You may be advised of pre-determined presenters or you may have to source them. When a keynote presenter has been chosen, research that person thoroughly. If possible, have a personal recommendation from a reliable source who has heard them do a presentation, reference check them, prepare a brief of what they are expected to deliver. This should be done before making a commitment and signing a contract. Knowing what you will get in the presentation is very important.

> **Example:** a conference selected a well recommended keynote speaker. A member of the team had heard the speaker at a sports dinner and found him excellent and very funny.
>
> He was asked to do the same presentation but, unfortunately, it was to an all-female business audience at 9 a.m. The subject matter meant he was not well received by that audience, leaving all parties feeling uncomfortable. This situation highlighted the importance of understanding the audience's expectations and choosing the right speaker for the right slot. That same speaker also was the MC for the remainder of the conference and did this very well. His presentation may well have also worked perfectly at the Gala Dinner for the same conference.

The right keynote speaker can be one of your most valuable tools to promote your event. Additionally, they may also assist through promoting your event themselves, so ensure they have any appropriate promotional material you have developed.

Other speakers

Other speakers may have to be found or they may be pre-determined. It is preferable that these speakers also be personally recommended. Reference checking and internet searches are ways to check that they are suitable for your event.

Either way ensure all speakers are well briefed on:

- the theme for the event

- why they have been selected to speak

- the topic area they are expected to speak on

- how long they should speak for

- day of speaking

- time they must arrive prior to speaking

- whether they are invited to the whole event or solely for their presentation

- number of attendees expected and then confirmed

- target group for attendees (i.e. engineers, medical practitioners, administrative professionals, in-house or external)

- whether they will be recorded (audio, visual)

- evaluation processes you are using

- any hard sell restrictions (e.g. can they put a plug in for their book?)

- who else is speaking and their topic to prevent content double-ups

- what written material they should be providing including what happens to their material e.g. does it go onto a website after the event?

When signing a contract for a speaker (see example Appendix C), ensure it includes:

- fee for the presentation, if any

- travel expectations
  - business or economy
  - direct or with stopovers
  - air or road
  - departure and return destinations and dates
  - whether there is a maximum cost for their travel
  - who is to purchase tickets
  - at special or full price
  - luggage allowance (do they have extra for their presentation?)

- accommodation
  - which hotel
  - single or double room
  - including or excluding which meals

- • number of nights

- • who will book it

- other expenses

  - • transfers

  - • health and possession insurance

- timing of presentation

- a list of speaker requirements for the speaker to complete and return (see Appendix C)

- Any other items that might be relevant, e.g. whether the speaker's partner might be joining him/her and what expenses for them might be covered.

Who is attending?

You need to consider:

- Who is your target audience?

- Is this event solely for internal staff, or is it open to the wider public?

- What is going to make people attend – relevant and engaging speakers, a point of interest such as prizes, food, free gifts, or networking opportunities with the other attendees?

- Are those who are likely to attend going to be attracted by the key note speaker, venue and/or location?

Once you are clear who is to be targeted and how many are expected to attend, then look at how many you should approach/invite to achieve the required number for your event to either break even financially and/or meet any other targets that have been set.

> **Example:** to cover costs if 80 paying attendees are required, you may need to send your marketing information to 100, 300, or 1000 people to ensure that 80+ attend.

You need to know whether the attendees are going to pay a registration fee or if it is to be free. If they are to pay, what might the registration costs look like and what might they include? Researching similar events will help you price your event to the market.

Determine how people will register – internet, phone, or paper forms with payment by direct credit, credit card, PayPal (or similar), or other means. Ready access to the registration processes may impact on registration numbers – if it is complicated it may "turn people off". Consider early bird registration, this can provide an enticement to potential attendees and assists the event organiser to have an idea of numbers attending leading up to the event.

Will they register and pay prior to the event or pay on the day? Payment on the day may allow extra people to attend but it can be the cause of a great deal of uncertainty for the organisers and lack of commitment on the part of attendees.

How should we promote the event?

Look carefully at how your event is to be promoted. The type of promotion will be determined by the target audience. For example, if it is an event for retired people then social media may most likely not be suitable but if it is for young working people then social media may be the best, possibly the surest option.

Promotion may be very simple, e.g. if this is an annual event for your organisation it may only need the staff to be reminded of the date and the venue with updates on programme content (e.g. speakers, activities, social events, etc.).

If this event is an open invitation to the public then consideration must be given to what advertising or marketing will be required, whether social media should be used and, if so, what and how. If previous events of this type have been undertaken in your organisation then the event folder will provide a starting point; however, this aspect might require specialist help.

If attendees are going to be paying to attend, marketing needs a great deal of thought and attention very early on. Determine a marketing strategy, perhaps seek help with this from either a PCO or a PR company. If the target audience is a clearly defined group of people, i.e. administrative professionals, then determine how best to contact them (maybe through their professional association(s)) and ensure this publicity gains their interest and attention.

Seek help from others who have done this in the past and use your networks to gather as much information as possible. Use all the mediums available to you to spread the word ensuring the information is out there as early as possible. You can add to your database through seeking expressions of interest, social media reminders and updates on progress. Use these as an initial mailing list for subsequent mailings.

Information can always be included as it comes to hand but get an initial set of facts out there – theme, venue, date, and initial promotional information on why they should attend. Add the remaining information as soon as it is available and this will include registration costs, speakers (especially a keynote speaker if one is being used), etc.

Waiting until everything is finalised means it will be too late to attract the maximum number of attendees possible. People respond best to continuous reminders, each with extra information.

> **NOTE** If you don't have an audience or attendees, no amount of planning of speakers, activities and all the other steps will make any difference.
> Identifying your audience early on will ensure maximum exposure of the marketing plan.

Media or not?

This is the time to ask if the media is to be involved in the actual event – are they to be invited, will they be interested, do they need to be prepared with media releases prior to the event? If the media is involved, seeking the help of a PR expert either internally or externally may be the best plan. Handling the media well and appropriately can be critical to your organisation.

Event timing and location

The date of the event and therefore the amount of time you have available to arrange your event is critical at this stage. How long until this event is scheduled: is there enough time to promote this event? You might need to consider if there are more appropriate days of the week to schedule the event. For example, perhaps avoid Monday day-time and Friday nights as these are often busy times for people at work. Or, depending on your market, consider avoiding school holidays as those people with children may take time off work and so may not be available to attend.

Alongside the date of your event is the location – is the event to be in:

- a major city

- a resort or holiday location (attractive to those who want to holiday before or after)

- a central local site (easy transport)

- a specialist event centre (good and easy facilities)

- a hotel?

The answers to the options listed above will determine many of the discussions in the next phase of this process.

> **NOTE** In some countries, there may be local government support (perhaps a percentage of the costs) if a large event is brought to their region. Alternatively, the support might be provision of information and introductions to venues in their area. Local knowledge can make a significant difference, especially if your event comes from outside that region.

What venue?

There may be no choice of venue, there may be an expectation that you will select a venue or there may be an expectation that you will provide three venue options for the event sponsor or others to decide. Ask questions and be very clear what type of venue is being looked for and in what location (the local area, the wider area or out of area).

Be prepared to discuss and negotiate with the venue providers in this early phase. When you are seeking quotes from several venues let them all know that you are doing so. This signals to them that this is a competitive situation.

When seeking quotes, ensure that each potential venue receives the same information and ask that they present their responses per those requirements – it is much easier to compare apples with apples than with oranges. Your organisation may have a template for "Requests for Proposals" (RFPs), in which case use one of those as this ensures that all information provided by those quoting is in the same format. It is hard to compare information if each quote is based on slightly different information, and unpicking each quote to get clarity is time consuming.

This is an occasion when a spreadsheet may be very useful for tracking the quoted information by venue. When recording the quoted information, be sure to note anything special or extra offered by any venue that perhaps isn't included in any of the others and whether that "extra" is of value to your event. This type of recording will make comparisons clearer and be helpful if the information is to be provided for someone else to make the decision.

Gather all the information about the venue(s) and put this information together into a report, called a "Venue Evaluation". This report can be used to seek approval for the recommended venue. Make sure all information about each venue is included, and that the report sets out advantages and disadvantages of each venue. This report is an important part of the event audit trail.

It is important that the choice of venue be confirmed as soon as possible, so your team is working with a known quantity and can start to build relationships with the event manager at the venue.

> Building a strong relationship with the venue event manager can make a significant difference to the success of any event, particularly if there are last minute challenges.

Sponsorship?

Determine whether your event is one where sponsors may be attracted and whether sponsorship is appropriate. A purely internal event, for example, may not be appropriate for sponsorship but a large event where considerable sponsorship is being sought may require professional sponsorship help.

Professional sponsorship help will attract charges. It may mean a set fee plus a percentage of the sponsorship secured is paid to the professional sponsorship contractor, therefore be certain to specify what the basis of such a percentage payment is. Be very careful that all parties understand whether the monetary value of "goods/services in kind" attracts a percentage payment or not.

Note that only sponsorship gained by the sponsorship contractor will attract a percentage payment and not any sponsorship gained by other members of your team.

However, the amount of money a specialist sponsorship contractor can raise may be significantly larger than that gathered using an in-house person and may therefore be worth it.

Also, remember that raising sponsorship can be a full-time job on its own so trying to do it as well as manage the event may mean your team's skills are spread too thinly. If you have a reasonable size team of people, then maybe one person could be allocated the task of sponsorship, but remember that if significant sponsorship is required, this can be a full-time role.

Discuss the benefits your event can provide to sponsors. Develop packages for at least two different levels to offer to potential sponsors. Discuss how acknowledgment of sponsors during your event will occur and in any pre- or post-event communications. Sponsors mostly want exposure so understand what that means to each sponsor and consider how you can best meet that.

Warning: Never include anticipated sponsorship into the budget. Record sponsorship on a separate spreadsheet which feeds or links *only the total confirmed amount* into the budget – this is a real "red flag" danger area if it is not managed very carefully.

In addition, be very careful of "in kind" or "goods" sponsorship. A sponsor may give the event items to go into a "goodie bag". They may wish to put a monetary value on this. This monetary value may be useful in allocating status to your sponsor (e.g. Gold, Silver or Bronze) but generally goods will not have any impact on your income for your budget so must not be included on that spreadsheet.

However, if you have a budget item and amount for "conference bags" and a sponsor donates bags that can be used instead of having to purchase some, then this would have a positive effect on your budget as you would not need to spend that amount. Or, where audio visual (AV) is a separate fee from the venue, providing this equipment free or at a reduced amount is another area where "services or goods" may have a positive effect on the finances; just be very clear and careful how it is recorded.

Event insurance?

A final question to ask: is insurance important or required for the event? This might include public liability, professional indemnity, employer's liability and/or event specific insurance (cancellation). This is an area where seeking advice internally and externally (including insurance providers) is important so that you can make informed decisions about what is required for this event in this location and per the requirements of your company and country.

Do not forget that an event where there are paying attendees might have different insurance requirements from an event which is being developed in-house for a company's own employees and is held on site. Clarifying the type of event is crucial to the information you require from potential insurers.

Timeline

This is the time to develop your timeline (see Appendix B) using whatever method best suits. A small event might be manageable using a calendar (manual or electronic with task list); while for a larger event a spreadsheet may be sufficient. However, for a large event, using the project management software used within your organisation might be preferred. Project management software is particularly good for managing pre-requisites or dependencies (where one task relies on another task being completed e.g. printing the programme relies on all speakers and activities being confirmed). You need to select a method which best suits your individual situation.

Developing a timeline is an excellent way of determining the details of every step or task required. Brainstorming with your team is an effective way to determine every possible task that is required. Perhaps record these on Post-it notes and then place these in priority order. Be sure to stop often and check that there is a logical flow to these tasks. Be careful to involve everyone on your team and listen to what they say.

Once your timeline tasks are agreed:

- allocate a length of time and a date of completion for each task

- allocate individual tasks to the members of your team

- agree milestones and review points.

Then enter everything into your timeline. A simple spreadsheet, as given in Appendix B, makes an excellent timeline where you can record all the tasks agreed at the brainstorming session. Along the top are the dates when steps must be achieved, along the left-hand axis are listed all the tasks required. Make sure that where a task relies on another task to be completed (there is a dependency) that this is shown perhaps through colour coding. Review points might be monthly to start, then weekly and finally perhaps daily.

The timeline becomes your "To Do List". In the body of the spreadsheet allocate a person to each task and show its completion date; colour code each person and 'the team' so that it is clear who is responsible for what. This is the time to ensure that everyone has input and so takes ownership of their tasks as allocated. The spreadsheet can also show overload for individuals in your team so this can be changed or at the very least managed appropriately.

It may seem unnecessary if there is a team of just you and the event sponsor. However, having that date for completion of each task is extremely helpful, remember you must ensure someone else can take over if you are suddenly not available.

Put your spreadsheet on a large piece of paper up on a wall. It is critical that it is kept up to date.

Example: In some earlier large IT projects, which spanned a considerable time-period, the Gantt Chart or timeline was printed on several sheets of paper which were stuck together and put up on a wall for everyone to follow. These were regularly updated, demonstrating how important the timeline was.

Your timeline should be available to all members of your team and reviewed at every team meeting. These meetings might be spaced out at the very start (perhaps monthly at the longest) but they will be more frequent as implementation time approaches. Weekly meetings may be advantageous as planning gains momentum and then even daily towards the actual event date.

NOTE Communication is a critical aspect of event management. Be sure that all those involved are kept within the loop, are invited to meetings, included in emails, asked for comments and input and have access to the timeline. Develop an environment where every team member feels they can comment on anything and raise any issues, particularly with the event manager and that they will be listened to.

At this stage, gather detailed quotes from venues for refreshment options and charges. Some of the venue quotes may list items on a per head cost for refreshments; others may list a total event cost per day for event room hire including refreshments. You may not be the person who makes the final decisions on these items, but whoever the decision maker is they will need all the information clearly set out for them.

Sometimes you may be told which venue is to be used; however, you still need to know what the costs are for your budget and to confirm the final invoicing is correct.

If you are providing quotes to the event sponsor, do your research well. Clarify how many quotes the event sponsor wants to select from, present the information formally in writing (using the reporting format from within your organisation) and, if appropriate, make a recommendation giving the reasons why.

Budgeting

Develop the budget spreadsheet for your event. Even if it is a small in-house event where a maximum figure to be spent has been specified and there are no registration fees, still create a budget to ensure expenses can be tracked.

If developing a budget is not your or your team's strength, ask for help. Gather the information such as expected costs for the venue, speakers, food, AV requirements, etc. and take that to your organisation's financial department. Ask for help to create a spreadsheet with appropriate formulae to assist you with managing the expenses and income.

An important note here is that if the country your event is to be held in has a tax on goods and services, be very clear how you manage this in your budgeting and your registration fee. Be sure to check out if, when and how this should be handled. Make sure that you have a column in your spreadsheet which records this tax so that it is clear. This type of tax is not part of your income or profit, it must be paid out to the tax authorities and so must be shown clearly. An easy mistake to make is to have some figures including the tax and some excluding it; this quickly leads to confusion and significant financial errors.

If your event is to be self-funding and perhaps even make a profit, then develop the budget very early on to support determining the registration fee to be charged and how many attendees you require to break-even.

> **Example:** if it has been calculated that the break-even figure for the event is 70 but 100 attendees register; all registrations beyond 70 will therefore be profit excluding any fixed costs.

Using appropriate formulae in your spreadsheet will allow changes to the figures such as expenses and attendee numbers and will show how that affects the bottom line. Once the spreadsheet has been set up, enter the anticipated costs and the anticipated number of attendees. Where anticipated costs have been entered once these become a firm quote, change them to match the quote so that there is a constantly updated budget to ensure the financial position is clear.

In your budget spreadsheet have an 'actuals' column which is only used once you receive the actual costs (usually an invoice), and for the final number of attendees (from the registration database) being sure to distinguish between paying and non-paying. Entering these actual figures will provide an accurate picture of income and expenditure for your event.

Retain the original budget figures as a separate column in your spreadsheet. This will allow variations to be calculated providing an accurate picture of costs for the event and highlighting where costs exceeded or were under the budgeted figures. These figures can help for the next event of a similar type that may be run.

Where sponsorship is to be sought and received, be sure **never** to enter sponsorship into the budget spreadsheet until you have a confirmed and signed deal, preferably only when the money has been deposited in the bank. Sponsorship can be a lifeline to an event where the number of attendees and their registration fees are uncertain but including it in anticipation is a recipe for financial disaster.

To monitor sponsorship, set up a separate spreadsheet page for sponsorship with one column for anticipated sponsorship, one for agreed sponsorship and a third for fully paid sponsorship. Only the total of that paid column should then link to the budget spreadsheet line for sponsorship. This means that sponsorship received is managed but only the actual figure paid will show in the budget spreadsheet.

Remember - Do not record sponsorship money in the budget until it is a confirmed amount, preferably actually paid.
Record promised sponsorship separately so you can keep track of it. Do not count on sponsorship to "break-even", it is best considered as the "icing on the cake".

Programme

The programme may be someone else's responsibility or you may be required to source information and provide recommendations. Always share information on what is happening, where things have got to and how the programme requirements will impact on your team's planning.

Find out from the event sponsor what their expectations of the programme are, who they expect to provide the information for the programme and when that information will be made available. Or, if you are responsible for creating the programme find out as much detail as possible about expectations and consult widely. The event sponsor will have some ideas for speakers, who can assist with information, what the theme is, etc.; you need to gather and record this information.

Expect there to be many iterations of the programme and timetabling and that it may not be completely finalised for some time. Put an initial "completion" date on your timeline but expect that to change a few times. However, if the content of the programme is not your responsibility, it is worthwhile defining in your brief that not finalising the speakers and/or activities in the programme early enough (give a specific date) is a risk and set out the steps required to ameliorate that risk. Be sure to get it signed off by the event sponsor.

Professional Conference Organiser (PCO)

You must promptly determine whether you require a PCO to help run your event, to manage the whole event, or if you require a PCO at all.

If your event is international and you are using a PCO, one who has travel linkages to manage the international travel of speakers or attendees may be useful. These are all areas that require consideration and must be factored into any decision.

Select up to three potential PCOs and then seek quotes from them. Select your potential PCOs through your networks and research. When going out for quotes from the three PCOs you have selected, clearly spell out what the quote is to cover, it might be best to use a Request for Proposal (RFP) which your organisation may have a template for, as discussed earlier. Ask all who quote to put their quote in as per the layout of the RFP. This assists with comparison of quotes.

Provide the same brief to each PCO. Gathering similar information from each PCOs quote will enable you to fairly compare their quotes –as has been said, "it is best to compare apples with apples not apples with oranges". A simple spreadsheet setting out the areas to be quoted on and entering the information from each of the quotes received will allow a fair comparison.

A PCO may have a set fee for their general event management services plus a "per registrant" cost for managing the registration process. There may be additional costs for special items –managing a themed gala dinner may involve decoration hire, table dressing, etc. Be sure to get all of this clearly spelt out and to require sign-off before money is committed.

Once you have selected your PCO, develop a formal brief of expectations for them along the same lines as the event brief you have developed for the whole project. Be sure to get their full costs spelt out very clearly and agreed to before signing up for anything..

Once a contract has been agreed and signed with a PCO they become an integral part of your team. It is essential you build a strong relationship with the PCO, meet with them often (this may at times be by phone) and expect reports from them at regular and pre-set intervals – all as part of their milestones in their event brief and noted in your timeline.

> **NOTE** Good communication is essential in your relationship with the PCO to ensure they know what you are expecting and you know what you are getting.

Gifts and Promotional Items

For some events, gifts for the presenters or others may need to be purchased, e.g. if it is an Awards event. Have a budgeted amount for each type of gift and be sure to source an appropriate item. Examples are flowers, bottles of wine, pens, novelty items or a plaque or other form of recognition. Take account of recipients' circumstances e.g. a speaker who had to fly in may find wine or heavy items impossible to transport, a speaker from another country may find the same, and seeds or plants may also prove impossible to take into their own country. Start arranging gifts early on so that it isn't overlooked and done in a rush at the end. Check on what has happened in the past if the event has been held previously.

Some events might involve promotional item(s) for all attendees. In some cases, this might be a conference bag, a pen, a cap or T-shirt, or it might be some other item. Promotional items will most likely be branded either with your organisation's logo or the event logo and they will often incorporate the year of this specific event.

A sponsor may offer to provide promotional items with their logo as part of their sponsorship agreement, again note how you might reflect this in the budget. However, make sure such an offer fits with the vision of your event. Again, checking what has been done in the past is an excellent place to start. There are companies that specialise in such items and it can be quite a revelation seeing what is on offer.

If it is an international event, gifts reflective of your country can be very appealing.

With promotional items your organisation might have a preferred supplier. However, if they don't, there are many out there, so do the necessary research to find out what is available to meet the requirements of your event. Select three or more suppliers each with up to three or more specific items and note the costings involved. Again, develop a spreadsheet to ensure comparisons are like-with-like and then seek whatever approval is required to select.

> **NOTE** If you require promotional items start this process very early on so that there is sufficient time to ensure the items(s) selected are available and can be printed with the required logos, within the timeframe. This is not a last-minute item.

Event Evaluation

Evaluation of an event requires planning to be undertaken right up front. Very often it is left to a quick "Happy" sheet on the basic organisation at the end of the event. However, this is not always very useful or meaningful. While the logistics of an event are important, a good evaluation covers much more.

Once you have clarified the objective(s) for your event, work with the event sponsor to understand what he/she wishes to know about the event and make those questions the first part of the evaluation sheet. First you wish to find out if your event met its objective(s) and then after that check on the speakers, venue, food, AV and all other arrangements. Sometimes there is great value in creating a pre-event survey asking what attendees might be expecting to have delivered. This can help with ensuring both your and the attendees' objectives/expectations have been met.

Creating an outline of the evaluation sheet should be done in this phase. The evaluation questions must be ones that will gather information useful to the event sponsor and your team. That information will be used to determine if the objectives were met, if there were successes and any lessons learnt. The design of the evaluation sheet may be updated as planning progresses and it is not unheard of for additional questions to be added as late as the actual event itself (although that needs to be managed carefully).

We know that most of those who attend a conference or event comment on speakers, food, venue, and AV more than anything else so put those questions at the very end. Ask the most important and meaningful questions up front. However, the skill is in asking them so that they can be responded to very quickly. Finding someone who has done survey work to help with this might be wise.

The evaluation does not have to be on paper, it can be electronic, using a resource like Survey Monkey with a link provided in an after-conference follow-up email. There is software available which provides electronic access to everything happening at your conference or event (for example Show Gizmo https://www.showgizmo.com/about), and you can use this to run the survey through attendees' phones or tablets (both Apple and Android) to provide participants' continuous feedback during the event.

NOTE It is important and valuable to discuss and confirm the evaluation strategy right at the beginning. To be valuable it must be planned with the outcome(s) in mind and not left to a last minute one-page sheet which deals solely with the logistics of the event.

Debrief

Set a date for the debrief meeting at this stage so that it forms part of the timeline being developed. Invite everyone involved, including those who join the team later, and have it in their calendars so it forms an integral part of the whole event. See Chapter 6 for more details on conducting a debrief meeting.

> **Example:** Set the date for the debrief meeting for at least two weeks after the event but no longer than a month after. The provision of financial information may be a factor which delays the debrief meeting, but make sure it does not get overlooked.

4

Detailed Planning

Once the information from your scoping has been gathered, detailed planning is the next phase. If the detailed plan is developed well, then the event itself will flow easily.

Venue

Once the type of venue is confirmed, talk with the venue providers to ensure you are certain what their price includes. Knowing what is included in the quoted prices, how it will impact the budget and the tasks on the timeline is vital. Some venues might have a "delegate package" which might be a per attendee fee covering all food, room hire and room equipment. Others will provide a venue hire fee only and everything else is added on.

Different countries have different standards so ensure you clarify what the venue is quoting for and what is excluded and if there are add-ons.

> **NOTE** In some countries AV can be an expensive external contracted service so may add a considerable extra cost. It is very important to be clear on this as it can add considerably to the expenses of an event.

The size of the event can impact on what is offered by the venue. For example, if AV is a separate cost and your event is large, a venue may offer AV at a reduced or no charge. If the venue is a hotel and accommodation is part of the package, this too can impact on prices or any extras they may be willing to offer. For example, a hotel where accommodation is part of the package may offer one or more accommodation rooms for free, or if the venue is at the hotel they may offer that for free.

Don't be afraid to negotiate, as many venues allow their Event Managers some discretion in pricing. As mentioned earlier be clear that you are approaching other venues as part of your negotiations.

Sponsorship

If sponsorship is part of your event, you should have made your decision in the scoping phase as to whether this is a role you or your team will take on or if it is something that is best contracted out. Be clear where responsibilities sit and whether your team have any role in gaining sponsors. It is a specialised skill but if it is decided to use a contractor, then that service will cost a retainer fee and a percentage of the sponsorship gained.

Sponsors are wonderful people who provide considerable help and support to a wide range of events, activities and opportunities. Sponsorship relies on relationships, on "who you know" and who can "see the value for them" if they support the event. It relies on you developing packages to be offered to sponsors at different levels and on your organisation's ability to provide value back to those sponsors. For some sponsors, value might be an immediate increase in their sales figures and for others exposure to a wider market.

One of the most important things about seeking sponsorship is not to promise what can't be delivered. Do not promise to directly increase their sales figures if that is not something that can be controlled by you or your team. There is an old maxim "under-promise and over-deliver" which is worthwhile keeping in mind.

> **NOTE** Sponsorship can be the "icing on the cake" of your event finances. It might ensure a profit is made, it might enable something extra to be added for the attendees, but until paid, it can never be guaranteed.

It is of course best, where you can, to get sponsorship offers in writing, but this may not always happen. Do recognise that sponsors can be unintentionally fickle. For example, they may have verbally offered the event $1,000 cash. But as events quite often have a long lead time, the person who made the offer may have left the employment of the potential sponsor and her/his replacement may not feel bound to honour that verbal offer. If that cash had been counted on and put in the budget, there could be a $1,000 shortfall which may mean two or three more paying registrants are required to regain that income.

As noted above seek offers of sponsorship in writing and record sponsorship promised in a separate spreadsheet with only the total of the paid amount linking to your budget.

Monitoring and Control

Careful monitoring throughout the process will ensure there are no surprises. It will enable you to maintain control of all aspects of your event. Reporting is a big part of monitoring and provides a clear audit trail.

Depending on the time available until your event, initially hold meetings at least monthly, these meetings should increase in frequency the closer you get to the event. The meetings are to review the budget, progress in all areas and on each occasion report to the event sponsor.

Include these progress reports as a line item on your timeline. Regular monitoring and reporting is a critical part of ensuring that everything is under control and that there will be no unexpected results or surprises.

If a problem arises with planning your event, first use your team to seek solutions. Only then take the problem plus the suggested solutions to the event sponsor. While your event sponsor may not always go with the solutions you have recommended, providing solutions shows that thought has been given to the issue and some ways to resolve it have been found. The event sponsor may have access to information your team didn't have, which could lead to a different solution from what was suggested by the team.

> **NOTE** Recording and monitoring progress will highlight any scope creep that occurs to help ensure there are no surprises. If something happens that might affect the financial budget or timeline, you need to report it immediately and then feed the change into the timeline. Never cover up such an occurrence in the hope it will work out, it rarely does.

Meeting with the event sponsor every time you complete a report is most unlikely; however, it is strongly recommended that you provide a written report for a clear audit trail. This is important: if something goes wrong, it can be reviewed and corrected more easily if there is a pathway to look back on and it is an extremely valuable habit for you to develop.

Programme

If you have responsibility for the programme – no matter how much or how little – you should have started working on this during the scoping phase. If you must source speakers, the internet is a good place to start looking. If speakers are pre-determined by the event sponsor, quickly seek their specific details and availability through the internet, emails and phone calls. Remember high profile speakers may be booked up a year or more ahead.

Official programme of events

The official programme of events may be pre-determined by your organisation. A rough outline of the programme may be provided to you with a request to "flesh it out and make it happen", getting sign-off as and when required, or you and your team may have designed and developed it.

Either way, once the programme is developed, ensure that the Event Sponsor understands the programme and their sign off is on the paper.

Contact speakers as soon as possible and get your event date in their calendars. Get a written, firm commitment from all speakers and let them know that you are depending on them to fulfil their commitment to you. For a high-profile speaker, you might consider including in their contract that they will provide a recommended alternative if they are unable to fulfil their obligations to you.

Develop a speaker's information form, which is sent out to them. An example form is provided in Appendix C. This form will allow you to gather critical information from the speakers as soon as possible so that you know their needs and can provide the equipment they require to do their job.

For high-profile international speakers, booking them 12 months prior may be required, though those in specialised areas may have different expectations. Once they are confirmed as available, determine how they will travel to the venue, when they need to arrive, what equipment they require, etc. Experienced speakers will have this information at their fingertips and their responses will provide a guide for you with other speakers.

Develop a contract for them to sign which should set out:

- what they are being paid for their services (fee, travel, accommodation, food, expenses, etc.)

- what will be provided for them to make their presentation

- what the organisation expects from them (date their presentation is due, format of their presentation, that they will be there the day before, etc.).

> **NOTE** This contract will likely require development by your organisation. Sign-off may be by the event sponsor unless you have been given appropriate delegated signing authority.

Official opening and closing

If there is to be an official opening gather as many details as possible of what is expected. This may come from previous events or it may come from your event sponsor.

> **Example:** An international event, held in New Zealand with 150 attendees, was to be opened by the Prime Minister of the country. Her staff were not able to provide a precise time of arrival, just a short window of time within which she would arrive. Therefore, the MC was briefed to "fill the gap" until the Prime Minister's arrival. The MC had to be prepared to instantly cease her own comments, appropriately welcome the Prime Minister using all protocols of address, usher her to the lectern and be ready to escort her to the stairs at the edge of the stage on her departure. Much of this had to be slightly "off the cuff" so an experienced person as MC was required.

Consult widely to ensure you have all the information you need. If specific dignitaries are being invited check the protocols for this and ensure all specified time-frames are met.

Where there is an official opening, this may even be run as a separate mini event within your larger event, with its own timeline and milestones to ensure that it is not lost in the overall arrangements for the whole event.

On occasions, there may also be an official closing. This is usually smaller and with less protocol, however it still must be planned for, and where there are people invited to participate or to speak, the same considerations must be given as for any invited guests or speakers.

Opening and closing ceremonies may be subject to local expectations and culture and may be added attractions for international attendees.

> **Example:** In New Zealand, some conferences may have a *powhiri* or welcome ceremony presented by Maori from the locality or *iwi* (tribe). This involves negotiating and agreeing with the local *iwi* what is involved and how this can be provided. This cultural aspect provides an added attraction for attendees who travel from overseas and want a uniquely New Zealand experience.

Social programme

For some smaller events, the whole event may be based around a social activity. For a large event, there may be several social activities which can be managed as separate mini-events within the larger event. These may be breakfasts, lunches, dinners, gala dinners, cocktail parties, etc. Again, researching what has been done before is important. This might be because it was successful before and a repeat is justified or it may be to avoid repeating something, not solely because it didn't work but because something new and fresh is needed.

Sometimes the social programme may include an activity such as a team building exercise, a tour of some local interest spot, a game of golf or perhaps an activity related to the theme of the conference. Again, these must be planned for and they should be set up after wide consultation so there is buy-in from all those involved in planning the event.

Often an "activity" will be run by an external organisation (e.g. cocktail mixing would be run by someone who has expertise in this and who can manage a group of people). It may involve transport to and from the activity which must also be organised. Once the activity has been decided on, selected and confirmed, this would largely be left to the expert contracted, or again one person might run this as a small separate event within the main event. Make sure that everyone is very clear what is being provided, when and by whom.

If there are a significant number of people travelling to the event and perhaps spouses, you may have to consider arranging activities pre-, post- or during the event to accommodate these people. This is one of the possible additional tasks that may present as scope creep if it hasn't already been discussed and a decision taken.

Registrations

Registration can be quite straightforward if there are no registration fees such as for an in-house event. You send out invitations, acceptances and declines come in and are recorded in a database. This is usually based on the database developed for the initial invitation mail out and from this you can print name tags.

Registrations can be more complicated if your event has registration fees or external attendees. You will require a registration form which must be accessible to the target audience. You may use the PCO to help you develop this or you may be able to do it in-house.

You may make the form available by hard copy mail or through the internet: links on your organisation's website, a PCO's website, or a registration management website.

NOTE If you are providing food you will require a question on either the invitation or the registration form regarding any special dietary requirements. You may also wish to ask if attendees have any special needs (access, hearing, etc.) and have a place on the form where these can be ticked or detailed.

Where you ask this information, you must record it and ensure those requirements are met at your event.

Developing a good registration form is a time to seek advice from other people. Find out how they managed their registration process, what their form looked like and how they got it out to their target market.

An example registration form is provided in Appendix D. With all registration forms, there will be standard data being requested, e.g. name, address, phone contact, email, company, etc. Do not forget to put on the registration form a breakdown, as appropriate, of the costs – is it one single fee which covers everything (specify what is covered), or are there some optional items?

If there is to be photography for publicity, it is wise to have a check box which asks registrants to "Please tick the box if you do not want your photograph to be used in publicity". You should then ensure that any objectors are not in any publicly available photograph. You might manage this by taking special photographs for publicity and announcing these before they are taken.

You must set up the registration recording processes that will be required very early on so that once registrations start to arrive everything is in place to handle them, ensuring none are missed or overlooked. As registrations come in record the details in your database/spreadsheet, including any special requirements that have been requested. Record payments and ensure receipts are sent out. If you are using a PCO for registrations, recording registrations is something they will manage.

PCO Financial Management

If a PCO is managing the financial side of your event, then they must have proper financial processes in place to ensure all money is held securely and that all payments are only made following an appropriately set up authorisation process.

Check how your PCO will manage the finances of your event. Preferably payments will be put into a trust account or other secure account, in case the PCO fails or goes out of business; in such a case and without a secure account, the money paid to the PCO may well be considered as part of the failed business and be lost. Alternatively, you could arrange for your event's funds to be paid immediately into a separate bank account which is exclusively for that purpose and is under the control of your team or organisation.

Whatever option you take, it must be clearly stated that at no time does the money paid to the PCO for your event belong to the PCO and that it always belongs to your organisation.

For financial security and clear accounting, the PCO's fees must be made on invoice and be properly authorised before payment is made. The PCO may not hold back money to cover their fees. This is a time when seeking advice from a financial expert within your organisation is valuable. Make sure that any contract clearly sets out how money is to be handled and that you are happy with this; have this checked by your expert in your organisation before signing anything.

Managing the finances in a transparent manner is a protection for everyone, you, your team and the PCO. Financial management processes need to be clearly understood and practiced by the team so everyone knows what happens to the funds and how they are processed and stored safely.

Pre-event information

Pre-event information for registrants can be important, particularly if the event is away from your own town or area. This information pack should contain:

- useful information about the area

- directions to the venue

- a map of the venue

- an outline agenda or programme

- dress code

- information about any activities that may be included and a dress code for these

- speakers'/presenters' biographical information

- information on when the day registration starts and what times the desk is open

- contact details for people who can assist the registrant (this might be the Convener or Event Manager or a "help desk" type person who has this task specifically)

- If your event has international attendees then additional information on medical services, shopping, advice on safety in the location near the venue, weather and appropriate seasonal dress, etc.

Objective(s) Expected

Objective(s) for your event should be agreed with the event sponsor and recorded in the event brief. If you are using a PCO these same objectives should be included in their event brief. These steps will have been completed during the scoping phase. Objectives

- should be simple and clear and therefore measurable

- are what the event is aiming to achieve and therefore are critical to the planning and running of this event

- should be at the forefront of all discussions and decisions

- may be used to develop the evaluation form to ensure they are met

- are what are reported against in the debrief report.

Evaluation

You are not always expected to evaluate an event. However, if the event sponsor wishes to determine if the objectives for your event have been met, then you must evaluate it against those objectives. Therefore, agreement on whether an evaluation is required and the type of evaluation required is important and should be sought during the scoping phase.

A post-event evaluation is a form of research which seeks the attendees' opinions or experiences of your event and you then analyse the data gathered. You may require help with developing the questions so that they gather the type of information you require. It may even be worthwhile doing a small trial questionnaire first.

Evaluation might be as simple as a one page or three-minute electronic survey covering the basics of venue, food, presenters and AV technology. This might involve a few questions with a simple 1 – 5 rating and is completed on the day.

Evaluation, if it is to be meaningful, is not something that can be done the night before the event starts. It must have a purpose, be against the objective(s) of the event and be planned so that it is integral to the whole event. This much more detailed evaluation to see if the agreed objectives have been met requires a more complex evaluation form. It would be worthwhile asking the event sponsor what questions he/she would like asked.

The evaluation might be paper based and handed out at the event or it may be electronic, for example an emailed questionnaire or Survey Monkey after the event or ShowGizmo during the event.

NOTE No matter what method you use to gather evaluation information, you must record it. Record the information in a database (again a spreadsheet will do the job), collate and analyse it and then incorporate that analysis in the debrief report.

5

The Event

Photo: 2015, 9th World Administrators Summit, Papua New Guinea

Event Run Sheet

Your "Event Run Sheet" (see the example in Appendix E) is one of the most important documents for running your event. This sheet should have every detail of what is to happen at your event including:

- detailed timings –when things are to happen

- who is involved –who has responsibility for each agenda item, contact phone numbers (always have a cell phone number) for everyone involved including speakers and the person who is looking after them, AV technicians, venue liaison – everyone!

- who will introduce a speaker, who will thank that speaker and ensure that the introducer and the thanker are aware of what their role entails.

> **NOTE** Introductory and thank-you speeches should be no more than 1 – 2 minutes; introductory speeches are about the speaker and/or why they have been asked to speak, the thank-you speech should include comments of appreciation and note a few points the speaker made –nothing else.

- photographs if they are required – who is to be in them, what are they for, when will they be done, who is taking them, who will round up those who are required for photographs?

- where the seating plan is held if there are meals that are orchestrated, e.g. for a Gala Dinner

- AV requirements for each presenter, for the dinner, for between speakers.

You are responsible for ensuring everything is in its place, is on time and everyone is where they should be but you cannot do everything yourself. Brief every person on the team who has a role during the event. Do this in defined groups – for example, a speakers/presenters group, those who are "looking after the speakers" group (be sure to introduce the speakers and those who are looking after them to each other), introducers and thankers group, etc.

Briefings may include the following:

- what is to happen

- who they can go to for help if they need it

- what their timings are

- that their speakers' needs have been met, e.g. AV, etc.

- introduction of each speaker to the AV technicians allowing time for them to check that their presentation is as they expect and is working properly.

If the event has been held before and there was a run sheet for that, then use that as the basis for your new one. Check through it in detail and add in anything additional for this current event, your previous experience and anything from the debrief of previous events which hasn't already been included. It is good to learn from the experiences of others.

This is the day that the good relationships you have built with the venue's event manager will be worth gold. If something unforeseen happens the event manager from the venue might be the person who can help resolve it. It is pretty much guaranteed something will happen, one of those risks you identified early on or something you never considered, such as:

- an attendee who has a gluten or nut allergy and forgot to put it on the form

- a speaker who wants to use their own laptop rather than the one provided by the AV people

- a speaker who has been delayed which you might be able to manage by swapping the speaking slot for an earlier lunch if the venue can manage that.

These are all very common challenges for the actual event and there will be a variety of others that will occur. The better planned things are, the more opportunity there is to resolve these issues; the better relationships are built, the more people there are to assist in resolving them.

Even if your team is small, if there are several things happening, often simultaneously on the actual day, be sure you have gathered together additional help. Allocate them specific tasks so that you can focus on the most important things.

> **Example:** if photographs are required, create a list of specific groups, and allocate someone to be responsible for this. They need to gather together the people from your list of those required for photographs and take those people to the photographer. This is a time-consuming job and would take you out of circulation for far too long.

Timing

One of your most notable achievements will be keeping everything running to time. Be sure to start proceedings on time, brief the presenters well about how much time they may have and that they must keep to time. Be sure to allow 10 – 15 minutes at the start of each day for the Chairman/MC to give notices, health and safety briefings and recap of the previous days' events. This both warms people up and gives them time to settle in and be ready for the first speaker.

If your speaker slot is one hour, advise the speaker they have 50 minutes, allowing time for overruns and more importantly, questions from the floor so that neither of these adversely affect the overall timings of the day.

Use a timekeeper, which could be a designated person, the Chairman/MC, or a timing device as an attachment to the comfort monitor, so the speaker can clearly see when they have 15, 10 and/or 5 minutes' left. Have a pre-determined plan for stopping a speaker if they start to go over time.

> **Example:** A conference MC advised the speaker she would stand at the back of the room during their presentation. When the speaker had 10 minutes to go the MC started to move up to the front of the room along one of the outside walls, timing it to get her to the stage at the finish time. Her movement while obvious to the speaker was not at all disruptive to the audience and it was clear to the speaker that their time was up. All the speakers at that event finished on time.

If a speaker is going overtime and they ask if it is OK for them to finish the remainder of their presentation, generally your answer should be "No, unfortunately not". A speaker finishing late is disrespectful to the following speakers and will lead the Chairman/MC into many tricky timing issues. However, if some spare minutes between speakers has been planned for, or if it is just prior to a break it might be possible to allow the speaker a couple more minutes. There is a saying "Do not allow someone else's lack of planning and preparation disrupt your own good planning and preparation". This is a time when this saying is true!

Ensure breaks are long enough to allow attendees to use the facilities and to have refreshments.

> **NOTE** If your event is all female remember that the use of the facilities might be slow and so arrange with the venue to re-label the men's facilities so that women can use both – this will speed everything up.

However, do make sure that the re-start is on time. Some events have a specific piece of music which they play in the last 2-3 minutes of any break so that attendees get to quickly recognise when it is time to return from their break. Other events have helpers who they get to speak to each group of people and advise them it is time to return to the event.

It is critical to have a good relationship with the venue providers and caterers, providing clear instructions when breaks and refreshments are scheduled and to keep communications open during the event.

> **Example:** Refreshments have been delayed but your relationship with the provider is good and you have been advised immediately of this delay. This prompt advice allowed you to arrange for the Chairman/MC to use that time for notices before calling the break, helping you to continue to run your event to time.

Chairman/MC

This role is vital to the running of the day. The person selected for this must be someone who can "think on their feet", is confident in front of an audience, and can handle a wide variety of unexpected events. You as Event Manager must brief the Chairman/MC on what is expected of them in their role. They need some warning – at least two weeks, preferably a month. They need to be clear about the objective(s) of this event and must have all the details of each presenter.

In some cases, the Chairman/MC may be the introducer and thanker of all speakers, in others they provide continuity only. They must be able to handle things if a speaker finishes early and fill the gap smoothly, they must be able to stop a speaker if they are going over time. They need to brief the speaker on timing for their presentation and advise them prior of the process to be used if they start to go over time.

They provide the linkage between speakers and if the event is a conference and is more than one day, they will often provide a link between the days with a brief recap of the previous day. They usually provide information on health and safety for the venue and present any notices which might affect attendees e.g. parking restrictions, check-out time at the venue if it is a hotel, etc.

They often provide the "mana" or "gravitas" for the event, ensuring all attendees are informed appropriately and all speakers are comfortable. In some organisations, this role may be taken by a senior employee or it may be someone sourced externally. For some events, e.g. an Awards event the MC is often a radio or TV personality or some other well-known celebrity, usually local.

NOTE Your Chairman/MC should be chosen carefully, as they will set the tone of your event. Make sure they are well briefed and have all the information they require to do their role smoothly.

Registration desk

This is an important part of the implementation process and good people are required to staff the registration desk. The registration desk is where most attendees at the event will go for information and explanation of anything they want to know or do not understand; at other times, they will come to you or the MC/Chairman.

Manning the registration desk is a role that a PCO will supply staff for, at an agreed cost, or it may be handled in-house. This is an ideal role for those who are detail- and people-oriented. The desk needs to be open for specific hours and these should be clearly advised to all attendees in the information they have been provided prior to the event.

Even if the event is quite small it is likely there are printed name tags or at least self-adhesive "Hello" name tags available at the door. If the event involves registration or acceptance, then routinely there will be name tags. At a conference, often the conference bags and other items for attendees may be held at the registration desk as well.

All events should have a registration desk at the entrance to welcome and record those who attend. It is important to have more than one person (depending on the size of the event) on the registration desk. This is where you can:

- spread the name tags out

- hold the roll of self-adhesive name tags and a pen

- have a list of names to be checked off when people arrive

- handle enquiries

- check people in

- hand out name tags, conference bags/material

- deal with those people who came but had not registered, those who registered and came but had not paid, etc.

- rearrange the nametags – this looks neater and more professional than having big gaps, it also gives registration desk people something to do between "customers".

> **NOTE** Open the registration desk one hour prior to the start of your event and over the morning tea and lunch hour breaks on the first day. If there is day registration (for a multi-day event) you will require a registration desk open every day.

Conference Bags

These may or may not be used; they can be a useful addition for some attendees and a nuisance to others. It is each event's decision as to whether one is provided, sometimes an event sponsor will provide a plastic carrier bag which will work quite well. It is a receptacle to put the conference handbook in, if one has been produced, or other conference material, but make sure it will be generally useful. For example, if there are several items such as a notebook, sponsor's literature, business cards, then a low-cost carrier bag will be appreciated.

> **NOTE** Conference bags can be handed out at the registration desk or they could be placed on the seats inside the venue.

Conference Handbook

A conference handbook can be useful; however, it can also be a real nuisance for some attendees – another item to carry around. If you do produce one, then it should provide:

- the most up-to-date Programme or Agenda

- layout of venue with rooms for presentations shown (if more than one room is being used for concurrent sessions)

- biographies of presenters/speakers

- speaker notes or PowerPoint information

- details of activities that might be associated with the event

- sometimes an attendees' list which may or may not have contact details for each attendee

- information about the local shopping, medical centres, religious centres, and tourism opportunities will be useful if you have international attendees.

NOTE Check privacy laws in the country where your event is being held as to whether you can include attendees' contact details. It may be necessary to have a tick box on the registration form asking "Do you agree to have your name and contact details included in the Conference Handbook - Y/N". This can be a tricky area in some countries.

Some of the material in the handbook may replicate that sent out with pre-conference information, however, there is value in having everything in one place.

Speakers/Presenters

Briefing

Make sure each speaker:

- is well briefed on your expectations

- knows who the Chairman/MC is and preferably has been introduced to her/him

- is familiar with the venue, the layout of the room and the audio-visual equipment

- is comfortable that their presentation, if they are using Power Point or other presentation software, will come up on the screen as they expect

- is comfortable that the microphone (e.g. fixed and/or lapel mike) and lectern are as they require

- is being looked after by someone to whom they have been introduced

- understands any measures you will take if they go over time.

This may mean meeting with the presenters the day or evening before they present, at the venue if that is possible, so they can have a quick run through the facilities and you can brief them on your processes.

On the day of speaking a presenter may choose to be at the venue quite early before any of the attendees arrive. If this is the case, then you and the Chairman/MC should be there early too. This is a time when a speaker may choose to wander around and fully familiarise themselves with the venue.

Example: Arriving early at an event allows a presenter to check things through.

An international speaker had been briefed on the presentation expected and had provided everything she had been asked for to the conference organiser on time.

Then things started to go wrong. At the last minute, she was asked to remove a slide from her presentation – this request was very late, disruptive and led to some very firm words being spoken and the request being withdrawn. Her flight was delayed; while she arrived the night before her luggage did not arrive until late the next day, after her speaking time.

This unsettled her and additionally, at the time of her presentation, she found several things that added to her discomfort. The layout of the room left those at the back of the room disconnected, there was no "comfort monitor" (the screen that only the speaker sees of what is showing on the large screen) and so she had to keep turning around to check her screen thereby losing contact with her audience. Only a fixed or a large hand held microphone were available and this tied her to the lectern, further unsettling her presentation style.

This speaker felt very uncomfortable but all these things could have been managed very simply had she had an opportunity to check things through.

Introduce and thank the Speaker

The introducer and thanker may be the Chairman/MC or they may be separate people, especially if there are concurrent sessions. Ensure that each speaker is properly introduced:

- make sure that the person introducing them knows the parameters of an introduction speech, brief biographical details (short paragraph or two) and perhaps a very brief outline of the presentation (1 – 2 sentences), and that the introducer should lead the welcoming applause and thanked:

- warm thanks, two or three brief points of interest from the presentation and the thanker should lead the applause.

6

Debrief

Debriefing after an event is important and valuable. This is the time to determine if the event met the objective(s) set right at the beginning and for the event sponsor to provide feedback from his/her perspective, e.g. did she/he feel the event achieved its objective(s)? What did he/she think of the analysis of the evaluations?

As the debrief comes after the success of your actual event it can quite often be overlooked. It is important to involve the event sponsor in the debrief process, as without their involvement this step can be missed due to other pressures of your and your team's work roles. The provision of financial information may also be a factor which delays the debrief meeting, but make sure the meeting still happens.

As mentioned earlier plan the debrief meeting when you are developing your timeline, and include everyone who has been involved:

- the event sponsor

- your team (including the person from Finance who helped you)

- those who helped on the day; if they are additional to your regular team you may need to include them in the debrief meeting when you invite them to help

- the PCO, if you used one.

The debrief meeting is the opportunity to share experiences, highs, lows and lessons learnt. Those who have worked to put this event on will all have something valuable to contribute and so need to be given the opportunity to share their experience.

Get the debrief meeting date in everyone's calendar so that they all know it is going to happen and stick to that date. Do not rush or overlook the debrief as it is an important part of the event.

> **NOTE** Set the date of the debrief meeting for at least two weeks after the event but no longer than a month after.

Completing the finances

If you have responsibility for the budget you must ensure:

- that throughout the whole project you maintain continuous oversight and record all financial information as it arises

- that you make it clear to all suppliers, including speakers, that invoices must come in for payment, promptly after the event

- that as soon as an invoice is received, you enter the actuals in a separate column alongside the quoted amount. The comparison between these two columns for each item and for the totals will show whether your event has come in under budget, met budget or over budget.

If a PCO was managing the finances, then all invoicing they were responsible for should have gone directly to them and any that came to you must be forwarded immediately to the PCO. The PCO should then wrap up the finances promptly, complete their financial report and fully brief you showing the results; under budget, met budget, over budget.

If someone else is managing the finances, perhaps in-house, then be sure to immediately submit all outstanding invoices for payment and request a financial report and full briefing on the situation.

> **NOTE** Reporting on the finances and whether the event came in under, met or over budget forms an important part of the debrief discussions and final report.

Invoices

It is vital that when invoices come in they are immediately carefully checked, and if there is any discrepancy promptly contact the supplier to discuss. This is the time to sort out any disagreements relating to charging.

Request all invoices from suppliers (speakers, caterers, entertainment, activities, etc.) to be provided promptly after the event. Follow up within a couple of days of the event finishing. Once you receive an invoice it is important to pay it promptly, especially if you wish to use the supplier again. Prompt payment builds trust and a strong relationship with a supplier.

If your organisation has a policy of only paying on the 20th of the month, then make sure that your supplier is aware of that policy. However, do note that if there has been money coming in to cover the costs (e.g. sponsorship, registrations, etc.), then there may be no real need to hold off payments. Delaying payments only delays knowledge of the final figures and the wrap up of the event.

Evaluations

Collating evaluations is a time-consuming task especially if there are a lot of questions and if opinions have been asked for. However, to analyse the data collating is a task that must be done and time must be allowed to do it carefully. This may, for instance, be the time when a complaint which needs addressing is discovered, though hopefully it will have been dealt with at the time.

The type of evaluation undertaken will depend on the type of questions asked:

- were yes/no answers requested or were written opinions asked for?

- were attendees asked whether they enjoyed themselves using a simple rating scale?

- were there more detailed questions which were aligned with the project's objectives?

If the evaluation questions have been well crafted, collating the data will be easier and it will also make the analysis and reporting straightforward.

> **NOTE** Reporting on the evaluation results forms an important part of the debrief discussions and final report.

Thank-you notes

People who have contributed to the success of the event should be sent a thank-you card, note or letter.

Those who have been paid for their services will appreciate receiving a note of appreciation, this cements a strong relationship. This can be an overlooked courtesy in this very busy world.

If a presenter is not being paid, a gift as well as a thank you card, note or letter is appropriate.

Do not forget to thank your sponsors for their support and generosity.

Recognition of those who helped run the event, those on the team and those who did so voluntarily, is also very important. Recognition might be a certificate of appreciation or a small gift, but always a thank-you card, note, or letter. Recognition may also be through taking someone out for lunch or a coffee; for instance, if you used a PCO or if someone from Finance in your organisation managed the budget and financial side of the event.

Writing an article for any in-house communication media about the event is also a good way to acknowledge those who helped. Another way is to write something to each team member's line manager commenting positively on their performance and request to have your comments included in their performance review.

> **NOTE** Recognise people's contributions by sending them notes of appreciation, this does matter to those you are recognising.

Debrief Meeting

The debrief meeting will have been scheduled at the start of the planning processes. Make sure that you have included everyone involved, including the event sponsor and the PCO if you used one.

Develop an agenda and allow sufficient time to go through individual items in detail. Be sure to take notes as these will contribute to the final report.

The agenda might include:

1. Event sponsor comments

2. Feedback on

    a. Planning and preparation

    b. Implementation

    c. Finances

    d. Evaluations

3. Successes

4. Where improvements can be made

5. Final report

The meeting should be carried out in an atmosphere where every person can feel comfortable in expressing their view or experience. Criticisms should be an opportunity to learn something or think about doing something differently. Criticisms should not be perceived as negative but are an opportunity for improvement or creativity.

Ask that the finances and evaluations have, at a minimum, been pulled into draft form but preferably that they are completed. All members of your team will be interested in what the attendees thought of the event and whether the budget was met.

Final Report

You as the Convener or Event Manager are responsible for writing the final report. Write this in the style used within your organisation. Your report should be to the event sponsor and note that it may be shared with others at a senior executive level. Also, ensure your report is stored per your organisations requirements, not solely in your own workspace.

It is helpful to provide an executive summary at the start of the report which lists successes, lessons learnt and how things could be improved.

> Your event folder may well be used to support subsequent events so put the lessons learnt right up front where they are easily visible. This may help others in the future to avoid some actions, activities or events that did not work and to repeat those that did.

7

Real Life Experiences

1. Organising an Awards Ceremony

By Marion Lowrence, Director, The PA Hub

As someone who worked as a PA for many years, organising events became an inherited part of my role and fortunately for me I loved it. No 2 events were the same so I enjoyed the variety and it kept me interested. This doesn't mean it was easy; running events is often quite challenging. I have run the PA Hub Awards Ceremony since 2015.

Organising events can be complex and time consuming so having a plan is essential. If you extend this to an Awards Ceremony there are additional actions to add to the list you would not normally think about such as a seating plan incorporating evenly distributed winners throughout the venue. I was once one of 5 award finalists on a table (who I didn't know) with another 5 finalists on the table next to us. Nobody on our table won and everyone on their table did. We were known as the losers table and it wasn't a nice feeling. Even having 1 winner on our table would have been more enjoyable and we all felt extremely deflated!

Careful consideration and planning is needed for sponsors, speakers, ticket sales and the judging method to name a few. So where do we start? My actions list is extensive but I start with the why, who, where, when and how!

Why?

Firstly award ceremonies are expensive to run so check why you are doing it making sure you are not duplicating something somebody else has already established. Do your homework – check you can get the buy-in and be sure of what your overall purpose is being specific to your audience needs. Think about what outcomes you are aiming for and do know what your budget is. Award extras can add up quickly so be careful from the beginning planning stages.

Who?

Research your audience remembering it is better to have a niche within a dedicated sector so in my case I ran the Yorkshire PA Awards. This meant I was both job role and area specific.

Think about how your audience will react to an awards event. Will they want to enter and what kind of event do you think they would prefer? In my case focus groups and general conversations at our other events proved that the PAs wanted a more formal occasion with a sit-down dinner, speakers and entertainment. Things such as dress code are important confirming whether it will be formal or informal. A survey also works well for this. You don't want to be spending any budget unless you know who your audience are and what they want.

Where?

This is not just about choosing a venue although that is important; it is choosing the city, region and country. Make sure you can manage the area you choose. For example, if you are running a national awards ceremony, can you actually cope with the span of that? How will you invite nominations from more than one city? How would you market that? Be specific and stick to what you choose making sure it is achievable and realistic. Be careful on the location and check how people would get there? It may be a beautiful venue but if it is in the middle of nowhere does that limit attendance? Is there parking available? Are there sufficient bedrooms if people want to stay? The event space for the awards might be perfect but do ask to see the bedrooms and check they are the same standard. It is the last thing people will remember and that can affect your overall rating. Negotiate a special rate with the venue for overnight stays; this should be lower than the advertised price.

When choosing the venue, you **'must'** negotiate and never accept the first quote. Do shop around and enquire about inclusive rates. You will be surprised at how the additional items add up and before you know it you have run out of budget. Ask what is included before you sign any contract. I always make sure they include table linen, cloth napkins, staging, lectern and that someone will be there throughout the evening from the venue to 'go to' if any mishaps occur.

Ask how many staff are working on the evening to make sure they can cope with the numbers. Check there are enough bar staff as people do not like to queue unnecessarily. One thing that is often forgotten is checking whether the bar can take card payments.

Always check what drinks are included and that the coffees and mints at the end of the meal are part of the cost quoted.

I have known someone be charged an additional £4 a head for coffee and mints at a dinner for 300 and they were hit with an unexpected bill of £1200. Most hotels will include this if you ask and if not, do you really need the coffee at the end? Consider places you can save money and this is one of them. If you are having a drinks reception cost this up – it can be thousands of pounds if you are not careful.

Be clear on the layout of the room so it suits your Audio Visual (AV) equipment, sound system and vision. Make sure people have a route between tables to walk up for their awards. Visual effects are important – talk to your AV company. Simple lighting can be very effective as can black table cloths with white napkins and if you don't have a big budget, don't have chair covers if they are ok without. If the venue doesn't include table centres you can make simple ones – there are many examples on the internet or make a contra deal with a local supplier to showcase their wares.

Do check out setup times and breakdown times as this can be very stressful if an event is running in the room before you and you are waiting to set up. Be clear with the venue on your timings to set up and run through.

Make sure you have a contract with EVERYTHING written down including timings and make sure you read it all before signing.

When?

This is vitally important. Make sure there are no other awards of a similar nature or big events in your area at the same time. Be careful to check out national holidays, school holidays and major sporting events that may clash which can affect attendance or cause traffic congestion. Look at what day of the week suits your audience. With our Awards

Thursday evening suited our audience; Friday was not wanted by the majority due to weekend commitments.

Think about how long the event should be and whether day or evening suits best? I've been at many events when people have got bored as the Awards part was too long. Consider the timings and stick to them and take time to choose speakers and a host who will adhere to this.

Our awards timings:

9am–5pm	Set-up, decor, lighting, sound checks, presentation/music run through, final table checks
5pm – 6pm	Team to get ready
6:30pm	Drinks reception
7:15pm	Welcome
7:30pm – 9pm	Dinner
9pm	After-dinner speaker
9:20pm	Awards Ceremony
10:30	Live entertainment/DJ
1:00	Close

How?

What is your budget and what can you realistically do with this? Do you need additional sponsorship? If yes, what can you offer them in return? You won't get sponsorship without answering 'What's in it for me?' It may be beneficial to do a contra-deal as long as both sides have something to offer. Ensure that all contra-deals and sponsorship opportunities are sent out 6 months prior to the event. Once approved draw up a contract to detail what each party receives and include payment deadlines to make sure payment is received before the event.

Start small and don't waste budget on things you don't actually need. Less is more - be simple but effective. Sponsors like to litter tables; be firm if you want a specific visual effect and be clear about this from the beginning.

AV is expensive; have a meeting and go through your exact needs so you're not paying for unnecessary equipment. Simple staging and a lectern can be included by the venue and with a little effective lighting from your AV company it can look just as good. Choose your colour scheme (we use our company colours) and have lighting to match. Do shop around and get at least three quotes making sure screens are of good quality. I really recommend a run through in the afternoon to check microphones, music and screen information is all in working order and to let the band (if you have one) have a sound check.

Always take time to make a decision; don't accept the first offer for the sake of it. Carefully consider, negotiate and draw up a contract. Remember you cannot run an awards ceremony on contra-deals alone; you need hard cash too.

Remember extras such as trophies/engraving costs, certificates, table plans, card/envelopes for winner announcements, speaker fees, awards brochure, website production costs, overnight hotel fees, transport costs, band fees, PR and prizes for the winners.

Other than the fundamental steps for running events, an awards ceremony has extra things to be considered:

The Menu

Do you need special dietary requirements? Have a tasting before the event at the venue, choose your menu and take photos. Make sure everything is in the contract regarding the food and don't sign until you are happy. Be imaginative but not so it doesn't work on mass production! Ask the chef for advice.

Nomination Process

Can they apply online? This is simpler for you at shortlisting stage as it's easier to have applications in one place, especially if you can export into Excel. Is the application process simple? Be clear on application criteria and on who can nominate.

Have a launch date for nominations and a set closing date with clear instructions of the judging process. Is it an interview, paper based or a voting system? Give finalists enough notice of the interview dates, if applicable.

Be timely – remember ticket sales increase once finalists are announced.

The Judges

Choose your panel carefully and make sure they are relevantly qualified in choosing winners from the awards field they are judging. Have clear guidelines and have a varied set of judges who can bring different opinions to the table. I personally recommend an independent panel.

Public Relations (PR) and Marketing

Your winners can promote for the next year so if it is your first year make sure you are clear about this so they know before applying. Our winner does speaking engagements for the following year so they need to know this.

Think of PR around the event before, during and after. Can you tell a story about the event so the local papers will promote it as an article rather than an advert?

Social Media is vital for my events and it is free! Consider your campaign at the beginning and schedule time for this.

Do have a professional photographer as you can use the photos to promote the next event and preferably a videographer. Visuals will help sell future events. If budget is tight think about hiring a media student from your local university.

It is essential to keep a record of:

- Applicants

- Finalists

- Judges Decisions

- Attendees

- Budget

- Costs

- Profit and Loss records

- Your time spent

All this can be done with spreadsheets as you go along so you know where you are throughout the event.

However, after all the intricate detailing and organising of such an event remember it is a celebration. Don't lose sight of the reasons behind the awards. This is someone's moment - let them feel it and enjoy it.

2. Running an event when the earth keeps shaking

By Robyn Bennett, TeamLink Training Ltd, New Zealand

First published in Executive Secretary Magazine October 2016

(**NB:** so timely with a 7.8 earthquake hitting North Canterbury on 14 November 2016 which shook and damaged buildings in Wellington, the Capital City)

On 4 September 2010, Christchurch, Canterbury, New Zealand was hit by a 7.1 magnitude earthquake, which caused major damage in the city.

I run a business training administrators, and the highlight of our training year was the Southern Secretarial Summit, which I'd been running for seven years. This was a hugely successful conference that attracted over 100 administrators all round New Zealand.

When the earthquake hit we were six weeks out from running the Summit. Aftershocks continued to rock the city day and night. Some were baby ones and others forced you to take cover under the doorframe or a table hanging on for dear life while your heart thundered in your chest. However, Cantabrians were doing what they did best. Getting on with it and coping the best they could. Earthquakes would not dent our confidence or prevent us from living our lives.

One day out from the Summit everything was organised and we were on track. My PA and I had some things to pick up from the mall. We were in the supermarket when wham! The ground started shaking, shelves and lightshades swayed and cans hit the floor. The stress of organising an event under such tiring conditions had finally hit me. And there in the middle of supermarket I had a meltdown! The ground was shaking and I was shaking. It wasn't the earthquake itself that had bothered me, but it was the 'straw that broke the camel's back'. While my PA comforted me and supermarket staff offered me a cup of tea (tea seems to fix everything) life was still going on. News travels fast and within moments my cell phone was ringing and beeping as texts and emails were coming in. And they all had the same message – were we still having the Summit? We had just experienced the biggest aftershock since the 4th of September (5.0 magnitude, 9 km deep). Power was knocked out in the city and buildings were evacuated.

We had to make a quick decision. The implications of not having the Summit were huge, but we had to consider that this was a serious situation that ultimately could affect people's safety. We took the risk and let everyone know the Summit was still on and we looked forward to seeing them tomorrow! Some registrants withdrew even though they knew they wouldn't get a refund.

My PA and I checked into the hotel (on the 19th floor – gulp!) and wondered whether to laugh or cry at the torch beside the bed (to help guide our way out of the hotel in the darkness if the power went off). We were exhausted from the day's events, but still on high alert. I hoped and prayed that our Summit would go off without a hitch and the earth would be kind.

On the morning of the conference registrants arrived excited, but a little apprehensive.

At the opening the MC did a great job at explaining what the hotel required us to do if an earthquake struck. Take cover and DO NOT evacuate the building until the all clear was given.

At 9.30 am we had our first earthquake. Most people felt it, but everyone remained calm. And that, I'm pleased to say, was the only earthquake we had throughout the event.

What did I learn from running an event in a seismically active city?

Risk assessment plan

This needs to cover many things including 'Acts of God'. These will happen when we least expect them, but ensure that these risks have been identified along with the likelihood of it happening and the consequences if it did happen.

Back up venue

We were lucky enough that the venue wasn't affected, but having a back-up in mind would help if your main one becomes inoperable.

Group email

As you register people for your event add them to a group email. This way if you need to contact them quickly you've already set them up and with a click of a button the message is out quickly.

Health and safety

Make sure everyone has a clear understanding of the emergency procedures.

Cancellation policy

Ensure it's quite clearly stated on your registration information what the cancellation policy is.

Forward thinking and having robust plans in place will help you to manage those Acts of God that may happen in an event. As an event manager, it was a different experience and one I hope I don't have to repeat any time soon!

3. Running Executive Secretary LIVE Overseas

By Matthew Want, Personal Assistant to Lucy Brazier, Executive Secretary Magazine (ESM)

Organising an event always has its challenges. Organising one which is outside of your country has even more challenges. We learn something new from each event to remember and put in place for the next one.

For Executive Secretary LIVE, as a team, we all have our roles to play when organising these overseas events. There is so much prep work that takes place beforehand, months of planning, marketing, and advertising, etc. Two members of the team are solely responsible for the marketing, getting exhibitors, press and media advertising and getting the initial buy in from potential delegates.

Another member of the team is responsible for keeping the database up to date, the admin and invoicing for delegates, the speakers' travel info, passport details, hotel accommodation and transfers.

I, together with a colleague, am responsible for the contact and follow up of leads who are wanting to book for the event.

Pre-planning

During the pre-planning stage, we get in touch with the contacts we have in a region we are interested in holding the event. These contacts assist us and advise us on the current market, what companies and provinces to approach, what media and press channels are available.

Before an event is officially launched, Lucy travels to that region several times, research is done on what venue would be suitable for the event too. Once we have decided on a venue, we enter negotiations with that venue for costs of event, accommodation, etc.

Lucy then gets in touch with the selected speakers for that event and gets confirmation of their participation.

Once contracts/agreements have been signed with venue, shuttle transfers and speakers, the brochures and marketing plans for press and social media are drawn up and we start advertising the event 6-12 months prior to the event.

Marketing the event

Fortunately, before we started doing our events overseas, we had done one in London so our database was already loaded with the delegates' information as well as subscribers in that region. Each person is emailed individually with brochures, booking forms and business case letters.

Each person we have as a contact on our social media and mailing list, and who is in that region or the surrounds, is labelled as a lead until we get a booking from them, and they become a delegate.

Various special offers are run throughout the marketing months leading up to the event to encourage bookings for that event.

In some regions, like the Middle East, we learned, we cannot rely on the mails and social media advertising to get their buy in for the event. Those in the Middle East prefer a phone call and direct contact. Therefore, several of us on the team start phoning and getting in touch with those who have not responded and those who showed a keen interest in booking the event.

Speakers

Speakers are contacted beforehand for their passport information and letters of invite are sent to them too in case this is needed for visa applications, etc.

A month prior to event, we get their presentations and handouts required for their speaking slots.

Delegates

Once booking forms are received, delegates are invoiced, their profiles are loaded on our system for future reference and future events in that region.

Just prior to event, follow-ups are done to ensure all payments are received before they can attend the event.

Admin

All information for the delegates pack is obtained and updated so that printing can be done in time for the event.

We ensure that all invoicing has been done and that payments have either been done or are in the pipeline.

One to two weeks prior to event

Speakers: Joining instructions are sent out to speakers with agenda, networking events, airport/hotel transfer company details, hotel details, everything they need to know about the event, etc. Confirmation of transfers and reservation numbers for their hotel is also sent to them.

Delegates: Joining instructions are also sent to delegates with the agenda, networking events, hotel details and everything they need to know about the event, etc.

A day or two before the event

IT and technical details are discussed with the contact at the hotel to ensure that everything is set up and tested, ready for the big day.

Exhibitors are contacted and advised when to set up and ready prior to the event.

Setup of the room is discussed and planned.

Hotel confirmation and room reservations are checked and confirmed.

Airport/Hotel transfer company bookings and reservations are confirmed for arrival at the airport to hotel and again on departure from the hotel.

Day tours and/or leisure activities are confirmed.

Transfers to networking and gala evening events are confirmed.

The evening before the event

Name tags are printed and organised. Any stationery or other items required at the registration table are packed in boxes ready to be taken to the registration table early the next morning.

One of our team's most important tools during the event is using WhatsApp. We set up a group for the ESM team so that any quick requests are attended to immediately. This also prevents us from disturbing the conference by going to speak to any one of the team in or out of the room. This works very well.

The day of the event

About 1-2 hours before start of day one, the registration table is set up with badges, the book table with speakers' books and various ESM magazines, flyers, etc. is set up. Exhibitors set up their tables. A list is kept of who is attending what networking event at conference so that numbers are confirmed for each of those events.

The doors open and the event is underway.

We are on standby with roving microphones for any questions during the sessions.

We are on standby for any last-minute requests or changes. One or two of us remain outside the conference room to follow up on any last-minute details and delegates arriving late. We sometimes alternate between us, giving each of us an opportunity to go and listen to speakers.

Photographs are taken randomly throughout the event.

After the event

The day after the event the team gets together for a brunch and just to relax and recoup before making their way back home.

Back at the office, all information regarding delegates is updated on the system and made ready for the next event.

Conclusion

Working outside of your own town, country, or region has many more challenges. You need to build trust in the people you are dealing with that they will be holding up their end of the bargain while you are still back home. Constant contact is required to keep the flow going and the interest intact.

I am very fortunate to have a team that pulls together in crisis and is up to date on everything up to and during the event. We all know what is at stake, we all know what is expected of us and we just get on and do it. We have an amazing rapport amongst us and that is why it makes it all worth it.

Our team is always on standby for our speakers, transfers company, technical team, hotel, and the ESM team.

We hold more than one event outside of London – next year, 2017, we are going to South Africa, Auckland, and Washington DC. We have developed contacts in each of those countries who assist us with the marketing and logistics. They too form an integral part of our team at the time of the event.

4. Running an international event with a voluntary team – Stars 2000

NZSES International Conference & AGM and International Secretarial Summit, Wellington, New Zealand

By Tricia Caughley, Co-Convenor

Background

In 2000, the New Zealand Society of Executive Secretaries (NZSES)[1] was the primary association for administrative professionals in New Zealand.

---

[1]Now known as the Association of Administrative Professionals New Zealand Inc (AAPNZ)

From 1992, every 3 - 4 years, the International Secretarial Summit[2] was held, attended by delegates from international administrative professional organisations (AIOP(Australia), IAAP(USA), OPSA (South Africa), ASA(Asia), IQPS(UK), etc.). They meet to discuss worldwide administration trends, share what was happening in their region, and agree on a range of actions to be taken to support each other.

NZSES's bid to hold the Secretarial Summit in New Zealand in the year 2000 had been successful at the event in South Africa three years previously.

Initiating and Scoping the Event – Three in One

In mid-1998 the NZSES National Executive Committee decided there was value in hosting the Summit at the same time as the national NZSES Annual General Meeting and international conference being held in Wellington, the capital of New Zealand, early July 2000.

This was a very large event encompassing all three separate functions in one week from Sunday evening 2 July – Sunday lunch-time 9 July 2000.

- the International Secretarial Summit ran from an evening reception on 2 July - 4 July inclusive

- the NZSES AGM was held on 5 July

- the NZSES International Conference ran from 6 July - lunchtime 9 July.

NZSES members were full time employed administrators, so a very clear understanding was required of the time and effort from each team member and the complexity of working together on a voluntary basis. The value to the

2 Now known as the World Administrators Summit

Wellington NZSES Group members who joined the Stars 2000 Project Team was the experience of working on a large project, building relationships of trust and learning many tools and techniques relating to project management. It was a golden opportunity to gain hands-on experience in project work.

In November 1998, the three organising committees (the International Secretarial Summit, the national NZSES Annual General Meeting and the NZSES International Conference) were all formed from Wellington NZSES Group members and so the journey began.

A logo for the whole week, covering all three events was designed – *STARS 2000 – Stretching for the Stars.*

Two committees reported to the NZSES National Executive Committee (for the International Secretarial Summit and the NZSES Annual General Meeting), and one committee, for the NZSES International Conference, reported to the Directors of the NZSES Training Company. Fortunately, the NZSES National President lived in Wellington and was an ex officio member of all the committees; having that direct contact made some decision-making straightforward.

Eth Lloyd and I were asked to be co-convenors of the International Conference – 3 ½ days from Thursday 6 July to Sunday 9 July, 2000. (That's what happens when you have a delightful lunch outside on a lovely Wellington day with passionate NZSES members. They convinced us that together we could do this.)

While Eth and I had different skill sets they complimented each other and we were good communicators. We both had a passion to see administrators grow in skills and confidence and recognised that the conference would provide a platform to encourage people to gain new skills, have an opportunity to attend a relevant international conference and encourage new people to join NZSES.

From early 1999 to mid-2000 the Chairs of each committee met regularly to ensure that activities were synchronised, on track and each organising committee was aware of what planning was taking place in each arena. These were important meetings because the support was vital on several levels – project management, physical, emotional and mental – as stress took its toll on all of us.

Planning for the NZSES International Conference

Planning for our event started with monthly three hour meetings on a Saturday morning from February 1999. As with most groups, there was a "forming, storming, norming" process to go through and some people recognised that they couldn't continue and pulled out while others saw an opportunity to step up. Email was available but not to the level of today, but it was useful for communication.

We made use of all the brainstorming, planning, checking, revising, searching for new tools and techniques that project management utilises to assist us. Once we had a consensus for the programme we began the work: arranging the venue, inviting speakers, developing the Conference Handbook, and employing a PCO to manage registrations.

All the conference committee members had excellent administration skills, and some with high-level skills shared those, such as complex document formatting, contacts across their respective industries, access to sponsorship, and first-hand knowledge of good presenters and trainers. Portfolios were allocated to committee members per their preference and sub groups developed where necessary depending on the size of the portfolio.

There were several personnel changes mid-stream as personal challenges, job changes, family sickness and other unexpected events took their toll. The Financial

Administrator role changed twice until I took it on and learned how to manage it. I also took over the sponsorship role, learning how to talk to sponsors and get their commitment. You don't know what you can do until you **have** to do it! Sometimes you just must pick up the challenge and learn as you go.

We all worked together as a team through 1999 with monthly meetings. Early in 2000 we began weekly meetings as the pace of organisation increased. Eth and I shared chairing the meetings on a bi-meeting basis and allocated the meeting recording to someone else. These meetings were key to how the conference ran during that full-on week. We endeavoured to have inclusive meetings, encouraging active listening to others, the sharing of ideas and concerns and providing the opportunity for all to be heard with respect. It was a special time of camaraderie and learning.

The Budget

We were a voluntary group and so did not have a "Finance Department" to seek help from. NZSES's national Executive Officer was always available to give advice; however, we had to develop it and manage it. We started from a zero budget and built it as we went along. Initially we tried to work with estimations of cost but we quickly learned to deal with firm quotes, not assumptions. We had little money in the conference bank account from previous events to kick start us. Not-for-profit organisations can make a profit but the money must go back into the organisation. I was determined to leave something in the bank for the next event.

There was a lot of discussion about what registration fee should be charged. Many conferences in New Zealand at the time were charging over $1000 - $1300NZD for a two-day event, so our fee of $750NZD for a three-and-a-half-day conference was very reasonable. This covered: speakers, morning and afternoon tea, lunch each day and other background conference expenses for the whole time. The Gala Dinner was a separate cost for those who wanted to attend.

There were also several people the conference budget had to cover: the committee members, the PCO who handled registrations and arranged travel particularly for overseas delegates to attend both the Summit and the Conference, presenters including their accommodation and travel costs, etc.

All these decisions had to be justified to NZSES Training Ltd to whom we reported. Minutes of all our meetings were forwarded to the Directors and at times robustly challenged. The last thing any one of us wanted was to end up in debt, so the finance was a high focus most of the time. That was their concern and it had to be ours, too. (We did make a profit to assist the next conference.)

The Event

The week finally arrived! From the moment the Summit began on Monday the 3rd of July, until the end of the conference on Sunday about 2.00pm, the buzz was there. The enthusiasm of those attending the Summit spilled over into the Conference. We had the Governor General of New Zealand to open the International Summit and the Prime Minister of New Zealand to open the International Conference so there was a lot of protocol to be managed.

The Annual General Meeting was held mid-week which gave overseas visitors and others the opportunity for a free day in our Capital City, which put on her best dress for our occasion.

There were some stretching moments. One international group was defrauded by their home travel arranger who did not pay for their hotel accommodation, food or registration. This left this group in a particularly vulnerable position. Eth and I as Convenors decided to use some of our expected profit to cover their expenses, so they could stay and participate. Due to our detailed oversight of the finances, we knew we would make a profit and so could make that decision.

The evaluations of the whole week were very positive. All Committee members received certificates in recognition of their work and activities in bringing the week to such a successful close.

Debrief

The support of our respective employers cannot be over-emphasised as being vital to our success. It enabled us to step out of our work roles when required and do the conference. The CEO of Eth's and my employer sponsored the venue for a breakfast session at the Conference and requested all his Senior Managers to send their Personal Assistants to the Conference. On our return to work he was the first person to find us and say his PA had said it was fantastic and to congratulate us. That kind of sponsorship and support was invaluable.

Unfortunately, we were unable to have a face-to-face debrief meeting. The Conference Committee scattered in many directions after the event; one to work in the Middle East, one took leave to look after her sick mother, one went on a long planned overseas trip to visit her first grandchild, some changed jobs and it became harder and harder to get everyone together. We all felt that closure had not happened properly, it showed us how important that debrief is.

However, we all learned from the experience in terms of how to run and manage a project, and contribute pieces to something bigger. And we built a respect for each other as teammates and friends. Invaluable!

Appendix A

Event Brief - Template[3]

Event Name:	
Event sponsor:	
Event Objective:	
Start/End Date:	
Financial Year:	
Event Manager:	
Event Cost: (if applicable)	$
Approvals Signature(s):	_____ {name and position} Date: _____ {name and position) Date:

[3]Template from Huirae Management

Link to Strategic Plan: (if applicable)	

Event Background: (brief explanation of history if appropriate)	
Needs Analysis: (Rationale for Event if required)	

Risks or Issues: (Risk Management)	What risk(s) do you envisage the event may have? How will the risk(s) be managed?

Deliverables: (Key Outcomes, Quality Indicators, achievements)	

Milestones: (timeframe of phase completion)	Phase	Date of Completion
	Initiation	
	Scoping	
	Detail Planning	
	Monitoring/ Control	
	The Event	
	Debrief	

Budget: (if applicable)	Event Proposal Budget Attached/Hyperlinked

Event Methodology:	Insert hyperlink to Timeline

Progress Review:	Timeline dates vs Date of Completion	Achieved or Amendment to Milestone Required

Final Event Report:	Prepare a final report for the event, based on achievement of milestones, amendments to processes on reflection, any additional information to be noted. [Insert Hyperlink to Report or Minutes of Debrief Meeting]

Final Report Sign off:	
	_____ {name and position} Date: _____ {name and position) Date:

Appendix B

{Event Name} Plan - {Event Leader name}[1]

Week Ending	8-Mar	22-Mar	5-Apr	12-Apr	19-Apr	26-Apr	10-May	17-May
Team convened	EM							
Date Selected	AT							
Venue chosen	AT							
Venue booked	TM							
Flyer designed		AT						
Mailout database		AT						
Progress report		AT/EM						
Website arranged		TM						
Flyer emailed		TM						
Speakers confirmed		TM						

Task								
Bus Booked				TM				
Caterers arranged		TM						
Progress report			AT/EM					
Supplies ordered			TM					
Reg. Database set-up		TM	TM					
Reg Form/info			AT	TM				
Reg form on website				AT/EM	TM			
Progress report					AT/EM			
Receive registrations						TM	TM	
Speakers details						EM	EM	
Confirm caterers etc							EM	
Registrants invoices sent						TM	TM	TM
Progress report							AT/EM	

Name tags, lists etc								TM
Event run								AT
Debrief								T/EM
				EM - Event Manager				TM - Team Member
				TM - Team Member				AT – All Team
				TM - Team Member				T/EM -Team/Event Manager

[1] Provided by Eth Lloyd, Enderby Associates Ltd

Appendix C

{Event Name}

Presentation/Speaker Agreement Form – example[8]

<u>Terms of Service Expectations Agreement</u>

This is an agreement between {Event Organisers} and _____ in respect of the {event name} being held in {location} from {date}.

<u>Presenter details:</u>

- NAME
  ....

- COMPANY NAME
  ....

- ADDRESS
  ....

- PHONE & MOBILE NOS.
  ....

- EMAIL ADDRESS
  ....

[8]Form from AAPNZ Inc

Presentation information:

- LOCATION: {location and specific room at which event will be held}

- TOPIC TITLE: (will fill in as per individual details when emailing)

- TIME SLOT: (will fill in as per individual details when emailing)

Deadlines:

- A brief paper or your power point slides outlining your presentation are provided and these are expected to be available **by {date perhaps 6 weeks prior to event}**. Some suggested guidelines for your paper format are attached at the back of this contract.

- An equipment requirement sheet is attached to this document, please complete this and return **by {date perhaps 1 month prior to event}**.

Terms:

- Fee is $_____ excluding GST.

- Travel expenses .... to be covered as per verbally agreed

In the case of unforeseen circumstances, (event organisers) reserve the right to cancel the event four weeks before commencement, that is {date}, in which case no fee is payable.

For and on behalf of {event organiser}

Signed: Date:

Title: {Event Organiser with authority to sign}

For and on behalf of {presenter}

Signed: Date:

Title:

Equipment Requirements for Presentation at the {event name}

Presenter/Speaker's Check List[9]

Presenter's Name:

Contact No. (daytime)
     Mobile:

Session:

Session Time:

Presentation Date:

Room Layout:

The room will be laid out for workgroups (most likely utilising {actual seating arrangement e.g. round tables, theatre, lecture, etc – check what venue can do}). No delegate will have their back to the front of the room.

Plenary Session:

Date:

[9]Form from Robyn Bennett, TeamLink Training Ltd and AAPNZ Inc

Equipment Required – Please Tick	
☐ Data projector	☐ Large screen
☐ Laptop & connector cable(s) (*)	☐ If using provided laptop, please advise what software package you require _____
☐ USB Port	
☐ Flip charts .... (specify number)	☐ Laser pointer
	☐ Standard, manual whiteboard
☐ Microphone (please advise what sort, ie lapel and/or handheld and/or lectern)	☐ Power board / Extension Cord(s)
	☐ Video or DVD (please cross out one)
☐ Lectern	
☐ Television	
☐ Sound System	

Other Equipment Required:

....

....

....

....

(*) If using provided laptop, please advise what application(s) is/are required.

If you require anything in addition to the above, please advise, including dietary requirements:

....

....

....

....

....

PLEASE RETURN THIS FORM BY {date}

TO: {email address}

Format of the Written Paper

- Head the Paper with your presentation title, your name, and a notation indicating that it has been prepared for {Event name and date}.

- Papers must be available digitally with at least a 3 cm margin on all sides

- Length: Up to 10 A4 pages including references (guide only)

- Pagination, please number your pages as this makes it easier to refer to specific sections during the seminar

- Introduction: in your first paragraph, outline the scope and objectives of your paper and its relationship to the oral presentation (e.g. does it provide background information, or summarise the key points of the oral presentation for people to follow during the seminar?)

- Clear lay-out is particularly important as participants may follow the flow of the paper during your oral presentation e.g. use subheadings, paragraphs, etc. Bullet points and summaries are helpful.

- Plenty of 'white space' around lists and graphs enhances readability

- If your presentation includes detailed numerical information, this is best presented in your paper as figures or tables, to which participants can refer during the presentation. Similarly, use of diagrams and Illustrations may better explain complex information

- Appendices: Your paper can include a copy of an article or material presented in other publications (providing no copyright will be infringed)

- References: Please append a list of references you have cited or other bibliographic details that will be useful to people exploring the subject in more depth (optional)

- Be "visible" Include brief biographical details and organisational affiliations if desired, at the end of your paper

These criteria are intended as a guideline to help you prepare your paper.

Compiling the {Event name}

Your paper will be compiled, along with others and will be collated and given to all registrants at the time of registration. We need to allow time for clarifying, copying, collation and binding. Therefore, please send your paper by email to:

{Name}, {Title}, {email address}

By {date perhaps 6 weeks in advance}

Appendix D

Registration form - example[11]

{Organisation name and logo}

A. ATTENDEE INFORMATION
(Please keep a copy for your records)

SURNAME:

First Name: Title: (Mrs/Mr/Ms/Miss)

Please enter your name as it should appear on your badge:

Employer/Company/Business Organization:

Position/Job Title:

Postal Address (PO Box preferred):

City/Town: Post Code: Country:

Telephone:

---

[11]Form from World Administrators Summit, 2015

Home: Work   Cell

Email:

Special Dietary or Other Requirements:

☐ Please tick here if you do not wish to have your photograph used for publicity

☐ Please tick here if you do not wish to have your contact details included in the attendees listing in the Conference Handbook.

B. CONFERENCE FEES

Full two-day package – Thursday and Friday		
Attendees Name:		$000.00
Package includes: Welcome Reception, Refreshments, Lunches and Closing Dinner		
Activities (Sat afternoon – included in registration fee)	Yes	No
Golf		
Tour		

C. PAYMENT DETAILS

All payments must be made payable into **Xxxxxx Xxxxxxx xxxxxxxxxxxx (account details).**
FULL payment for registration fees MUST be received BEFORE the WASummit.

A confirmation email detailing all items reserved and payments made will be forwarded on receipt of registration form and fees.

Completion of this FORM will indicate ACCEPTANCE of the Terms and Conditions set out in this FORM and other Conference documentation.

I wish to make payment via:

Cheque			Please invoice my organisation
Credit Card			Please enter details below

PLEASE ALWAYS QUOTE:
Your Surname and Company for clear Identification

Credit Card Authorisation: (Please note VISA and MASTERCARD only)				
Please indicate the card type:	VISA		Mastercard	
Card Number			Expiry Date	
Card Holder's Name				
Card holder's signature:				

D. CANCELLATION AND REFUNDS

Any cancellation and/or refunds must be notified in writing or e-mail to the Xxxxx Xxxxxx.

Cancellation received in writing or email up to close of business on {specified period of time prior to event} will receive a refund less 30% administrative cost.

Cancellation received after {specified period of time prior to the event} will not receive a refund but a substitute is welcome without penalty.

Appendix E

Runsheet – example[1]

2015 AGM AND CONFERENCE AT THE {HOTEL NAME}, CHRISTCHURCH
THURSDAY 30 JULY TO SATURDAY 1 AUGUST
CONTACT DETAILS: {name}
Conference & Events Co-ordinator
DDI: Email:
Hours of work are Mon - Fri 8.30am - 12.30pm

DELIVERY DETAILS

Items sent prior to 21 July to go to:
{Organisation/Event Name}
C/o Xxxxx Xxxxxx {street address}

NB: Items sent after 21 July go direct to hotel: arrive by Wednesday 29 July to be addressed as follows:

(Organisation/Event name)
Attention: Xxxxxx Xxxxxxx
{Hotel name}
{Street address}

[1] Run Sheet from Marie Hucker, AAPNZ Inc, Life Member

ACCOMMODATION DETAILS

Suggest bookings that {organisation} is to pay for should come through Xxxx
Hotel Accommodation Co-ordinator: Ph: , Cell:
Rooms not required to be released by: {date}

DATE	ROOMS HELD AS AT 22/12/14	BOOKED	NAME	COST inc GST
30, 31 July & 1 August	1 Suite			Room rate as negotiated
30, 31 July & 1 August	1 room single occupancy			
30, 31 July	1 room single occupancy			
31 July	1 room single occupancy			
30, 31 July	30 rooms (single or double) to include The Award finalists			
30, 31 July & 1 August?	35 rooms (single or double occupancy) (extra 5 for 3rd night)			

RUN SHEET

THEME "ADMINISTRATION FROM A BUSINESS PERSPECTIVE"

The theme is around the need for administrative professionals to have business acumen, it's not enough to be working *in* the business, they need to have a better sense of *what* the business is about as well.

DAY AND TIME	EVENT/SPEAKER	LOCATION AND SEATING REQUIREMENTS	AV/EQUIPMENT REQUIREMENTS AND SPECIAL ARRANGEMENTS	FEE/COST/WHO TO CHARGE
		Hotel Event Co-ordinator: {Name} Ph: Cell: Email:	**Free wi fi in public areas and guest rooms** **AV provided by:** **Cell phone contact:** **Technician on site: {name}**	**$x,xxx.xx including AV technician**

Thursday			
10.00 – 11.00 am	Executive meeting	The Boardroom (8)	Room $140.00 (NET) 10 – 12pm
12.00 – – 12.45 pm	Lunch for Executive Team and Group Presidents	Camelot Room	Room $100.00 for 1 hr (NET) Lunch $23.50 pp(NET)
1.00 – 4.30	Group Presidents' Forum Representative from Xxxxx Recruitment to speak	Camelot Room (88) Cabaret Style 6 at a table	Hotel to provide: Lectern with microphone 1 Cordless microphone 1 lapel microphone 6' x 6' projection screen Table for AV technician	Room $300.00 from 1.00 to 7.30 pm.

4.00 – 5.00 (Last suitable flight from Akld 2pm – arrive 3.20 and WN 1.25 – arrive 2.10)	Registrations for conference and AGM Reg Desk: {Names} Cell:	Foyer	$500.00 from 2.00 to 7.30pm (NET) Registration desk provided free
4.30 – 5.00	Arrival Tea and Coffee/Cookie	Camelot Room	$6.80 pp
5.15 – 5.30	Official Welcome	Camelot Room	
5.30 – 7.30 pm	AGM	Camelot Room	Hotel to provide: as above
			Hotel will provide complimentary: Flipchart, whiteboard and marker pens Portable staging

9.00. – 9.30	Final registrations	Foyer		
9.00 – 4.00	Judging of The APAward	The Boardroom (8)	**Lunch served to judges in Boardroom. Tea, coffee and water to be available during day for the Judges**	Room $325.00 (The Award) 9.00 – 4.00 pm
9.00 – 9.40 am set up from 7.00 am	**Opening of Trade Exhibition**	**1/3rd of The Great Hall or Walkway**		Room $1,650 for whole of The Great Hall from 07.00 – 23.59
	Water, mints, pads and pens available on tables		Music must be played that is heard throughout the area	
9.50 – 10.50am (1 hr)		**2/3rds of The Great Hall (112) cabaret**	**Cabaret during the day, then it needs to be cabaret for the evening**	Travel and accommodation paid for – separate budget - Masterclasses

10.55 – 11.10	Short Break – Morning Tea/Cookie		$6.80pp
11.15 – 12.00	Second Plenary session Xxx Xxxxxx, Administration Manager, Xxxxxxxxx *Learning is a journey, not a destination* Email: Cell: Conf Contact: Cell:	**2/3rds of The Great Hall**	Gift
12.00 – 12.45 pm (45 min)	Lunch and trade exhibition	**As above**	$25.50 pp

1.00 – 1.50 pm (50 minutes)	Third Plenary session Xxxxx Xxxxxxx, {organisation} Email: Cell: Rock the Boat Conf contact: Cell:	**2/3rds of The Great Hall. 112 cabaret style**		$1,000 donation to specified charity plus travel and accommodation
2.00 – 2.45 (45 minutes)	Fourth Plenary session Xxxx Xxxxx, {organisation} Email: Cell: The realignment of New Zealand business qualifications Conf Contact: Cell:			Gift
3.00 – 3.20pm	Afternoon tea	**As above**		$6.80 pp

			As above
3.30 – 4.15	International Keynote Speaker - Lucy Brazier CEO and Publisher of TES, Marcham Publishing, 17 Wood Road, Shepperton, Middlesex, TW17 0DH , UK Cell: *Emotional Intelligence* Conf Contact: Cell:		
4.15 – 4.30 pm	Closing remarks, prize draws	**Venue - min 2 hr break needed between plenary and dinner to reset the room**	

6 – 6.45 pm	Cocktail function for sponsors and international visitors (if any)	**If Xxxxx's suite not suitable** **Den Bar lounge can do 30 for cocktails**		attendees at own cost – cash bar
6.30 – 7.00 pm	Pre-dinner drinks	**Xxxxx Bar lounge**		
7.00 – 10 .00 pm	Awards Dinner (see separate Doc) APAward Winner Speaker Cell: Conf Contact: Cell:	**The Great Hall**	AV equipment provided as above. **NB: AV supplier will provide music throughout evening**	$57.00pp Portable staging, Dance Floor Lighting – multi level adjustable, spotlights etc – complimentary

Saturday

		Camelot Room	As above
9.00- 10.00 am	Fifth Plenary - Lucy Brazier Marcham Publishing, 17 Wood Road, Shepperton, Middlesex, TW17 0DH, UK lbrazier@ executivesecretary.com Cell: Masterclass Social Media: Conf Contact: Cell:		Room $600.00 from 9.00 to 4.00 pm. NB: we only have one room this day so cannot break into separate workshops
10.00 – 10.20	Morning Tea with cookie		$6.80pp

10.30– 11.15	Sixth Plenary - Eth Lloyd Email: eth.lloyd@ gmail.com Cell: What value is a Qualification? Conf Contact: Cell:			Gift + travel and accommodation
11.30 – 12.30	Open Forum, Closing remarks	Camelot Room	Prize draws	
12.30 – 1.30	Lunch	Camelot Room		$25.50pp
12.30 – 1.45	New NET meeting over lunch	Boardroom		$140.00
2.00 – 4.30	Bus tour of Christchurch Pick-up Front Foyer at 2pm	Red Bus Rebuild tour with time at Re-start mall	Conf Contact: confirmed booking Cell:	$200.

TRADE EXHIBITORS' EXPRESSIONS OF INTEREST /AGREED

Company Name	Contact Details	Date Contract Entered Into	Items/Services to be Displayed	Paid
Xxxxxx Xxxxxxx	Xxxx Xxxxxxx Email: xxxxx@ xxxxxxx.co.nz Cell: Contacted AAPNZ via website	{Event contact name} – letter sent	Information technology services	$300 plus $100 extra to include lunch and dinner ticket
Xxxxxx Xxxxx	Xxxxxx Xxxx {address} Ph: M:	{Event contact name} – met 3/5/15 – sent follow up letter. Providing prize of 2 nights B & B for 2 people, subject to availability	Advertise B&B accommodation, wedding and conference venue	Quoted no fee buy breakfast or dinner tickets if required as alternative may be collateral in bags

Xxxxxxx Xxxxxxxx	To be manned by Wellington and Christchurch offices	{Event contact name} – see email		Agreed $500 which includes two dinner tickets – to purchase 1 further ticket
Xxx Xxxxx Xxxxxxx	Xxxxxx Xxxxx Managing Director Cell: Email:	{Event contact name}		$300 plus $65 for dinner ticket
Xxxx Xxxxxxx	Xxxxx Xxxxx National Mger for Xxxxx Xxxxxx Xxx Email: Cell:	{event contact name}	Photocopier, consumables and 3D Printer Agreed	No charge providing photocopier & consumables from Thurs am

ShowGizmo	Marie-Claire Andrews, CEO, Show Gizmo Phone: Cell: www. ShowGizmo.com	{event contact name}	Conference App	**No charge - national sponsors. Also breakfast speaker NET to provide dinner tickets**

Acknowledgements

I would like to thank those who have contributed to the information and preparation of this book, many of whom I have worked with over the years. It has been a team effort in many ways and I have truly appreciated the input from every one of you.

Lucy Brazier, CEO Marcham Publishing – for her innovative thinking, boundless energy, and decision that Executive Secretary Magazine should provide books which are "Guides to …" to inform and support administrative professionals around the world. For her initial suggestion for me to "Send a list of topics you could write a book on and then select one to write".

Leanne Fisher, former Chairman AIOP, Australia for writing the Foreword. Leanne and I have worked together on the World Administrator's Summit since 2003 and she has been the International Director on the IAAP Board when that position was in place. She has a unique and wide international experience of the administrative professional role and administrative professional associations.

Lynn O'Shea, Freshfields Design (www.ffieldsdesign.co.nz) for the graphics, working with Lynn is a pleasure and I am always happy with what she produces, from my logo to the conceptual diagram for my thesis to the graphics for this book.

Marion Lowrence, PA Hub – for her real-life experience of running an Awards night with some valuable tips.

Robyn Bennett, Team Link Training AAPNZ (Past National President, Honorary Member) – for her real-life experience of running an event when the earth keeps shaking, input and proofreading and for our times together in AAPNZ and since.

Matthew Want, Marcham Publishing, Executive Secretary LIVE with assistance from Kayleigh Morgan and Michele Thwaits – for the real-life experience of the tasks required and the teamwork involved in running an international event based outside your own country.

Tricia Caughley, AAPNZ – for her real-life experience of running an international event with volunteers, our time working together on Stars 2000 and other roles and her proofreading.

Marie Hucker, AAPNZ (Past National President, Life Member, Director AAPNZ Professional Development Ltd) – for her counsel when we worked together and her run sheet in the appendices.

Wendy Rapana, Huirae Management AAPNZ (Past National President) – for her project brief, her suggestions, and our time together on AAPNZ Professional Development Ltd.

Sherie Pointon, AAPNZ – for her valuable positive comments and suggestions in proofreading my early draft.

Cathy Forde, Dulux New Zealand, for her proofreading from a user's perspective.

Charles, my husband, for his initial proofreading and patience when I got a bit irritated at his suggestions.

About the Author

Eth Lloyd worked for over 30 years as a personal assistant holding roles in New Zealand, The United Kingdom, Bermuda, and Australia. Since 2005, she has managed her own professional development consultancy, Enderby Associates Ltd, in Wellington, New Zealand, working specifically with administrative professionals.

Eth has worked with many EAs, PAs and other administrative professional roles in many industries from government to the health sector, corporate business to schools. She supports them to successfully gain New Zealand national qualifications in Business Administration and/or First Line Management, enhancing their career opportunities.

Eth is a past National President of the Association of Administrative Professionals New Zealand Inc (AAPNZ) and a Life Member, with a passion for the administrative profession and their value in the workplace. This passion is shown through her commitment to assisting this sector of the workforce to gain national qualifications and internationally to take personal responsibility for their own professional development and career pathway.

To gain her Master's in Education (2010), Eth undertook academic research looking at administrative professionals in New Zealand, their professional development opportunities and career pathways from their perspective using their voices. Eth's research on this portion of the workforce was the first undertaken in New Zealand and one of only about 10 in the world. For a second piece of research, also undertaken in New Zealand, she won a Merit Award. These can both be found at http://www.aapnz.org.nz/member-benefits.aspx.

In 2013/14 Eth and her husband undertook a 12-month volunteer contract with Volunteer Service Abroad in Apia, Samoa, supporting the Samoa Association of Manufacturers and Exporters to establish a physical office. This opportunity used Eth's administrative skills and she was also responsible for training a local person to manage the office on their departure. She also undertook training as an ISO 9000:2008 auditor while she was in Samoa and used this knowledge as a basis for the policies and procedures documentation she developed for the association she was supporting.

2015/18   Eth holds the role of Chairman of the World Administrators Summit Advisory Council. She has developed an international team to take the discussions from the 9th WASummit in Papua New Guinea forward and to arrange the 10th World Administrators Summit in Frankfurt Germany, 2018 hosted by IMA (formerly EUMA).

Index

www.ingramcontent.com/pod-product-compliance
Lightning Source LLC
Chambersburg PA
CBHW050507210326
41521CB00011B/2357